TIME AND DESPONDENCY

Regaining the Present in Faith and Life

NICOLE M. ROCCAS

ANCIENT FAITH PUBLISHING

CHESTERTON, INDIANA

Time and Despondency: Regaining the Present in Faith and Life
Copyright © 2017 Nicole M. Roccas

Published by:
  Ancient Faith Publishing
  A Division of Ancient Faith Ministries
  P.O. Box 748
  Chesterton, IN 46304

All Old Testament quotations, unless otherwise identified, are from the Orthodox Study Bible, © 2008 by St. Athanasius Academy of Orthodox Theology (published by Thomas Nelson, Inc., Nashville, Tennessee) and are used by permission. New Testament quotations are from the New King James Version of the Bible, © 1982 by Thomas Nelson, Inc., and are used by permission.

ISBN: 978-1-944967-30-7

Printed in the United States of America

Author photo: Florin Pronoiu

25 24 23 22 21 20 19 18   16 15 14 13 12 10 9 8 7 6 5 4 3 2

For my husband Basil, my partner in time
. . . μείζων δὲ τούτων ἡ ἀγάπη.

Contents

Learn to master time, and you will be able—whatever you do, whatever the stress, in the storm, in tragedy, or simply in the confusion in which we continuously live—to be still, immobile in the present, face to face with the Lord.

—METROPOLITAN ANTHONY (BLOOM) OF SOUROZH,

BEGINNING TO PRAY (90)

Acknowledgments

As ONE MIGHT IMAGINE, DESPONDENCY IS HARDLY THE easiest topic to wake up and write about every morning. That this work came to fruition—and that I am still relatively sane—is in large part thanks to numerous supportive friends, family, and colleagues.

I would first like to thank my parents, Robert and Mary Lyon, for many things, but principally for raising me in a home where God—and prayer—are real. I am also grateful to my father- and mother-in-law, Constantine and Eleftheria Roccas, whose enthusiastic support of this project inspired me at times when it was sorely needed.

To the many faces at Ancient Faith: thank you for making writing my first book a rich and relatively painless experience. Huge thanks to my editor, Katherine Bolger Hyde, whose unseen work (and patience with my random emails) has made this book stronger; to Melinda Johnson, a perennial font of encouragement, ideas, and diverting guinea pig videos; and to the rest of the staff of Ancient Faith, who from the beginning of this project welcomed me as part of their team. Finally, to the growing community of Ancient Faith content contributors: what a wonderful, loving, and helpful network we have been blessed with. Thank you for letting me learn from you all!

Numerous people have strengthened this work indirectly. My gratitude to my friends and writing accountability partners, Drs. Sarah Bereza and Brittany Cowgill, for our weekly check-ins and so much more. Thank you also to Caleb Shoemaker and Dr. Elizabeth Wade-Sirabian for lending their linguistic expertise to select portions of this manuscript. Additionally, I wish to acknowledge a number of folks whose general encouragement has benefited this work in ways seen and unseen: Diana "Di" Carter, Kerry Fast, Dr. Sigrun Haude, Sharon Helleman, Mary Marrocco, Fr. Philip and Khouria Kathryn Rogers (and all the wonderful ladies at St. John Orthodox Church in Memphis, Tennessee), Kim Schneider, and Tom Windels. I am grateful for the parishes I have called home over the years for sharing with me the journey of what it means to be the Body of Christ in this temporal life: Metamorphosis Greek Orthodox Church (Toronto, Ontario), St. Silouan the Athonite Mission Parish (Toronto), and Christ the Savior–Holy Spirit Orthodox Church (Cincinnati, Ohio).

During the final months of finishing this book, I suffered a rather vexing bout of writer's block that lifted only a couple of days before my deadline, during which time I did the unthinkable and rewrote the conclusion of this book from scratch. Dimitra Chronopoulos: without that freezing, late-winter walk on the ravine trail, the end of this book would be a far cry from what (I hope) it has become. I'm blessed to have a friend who will tell me when to scrap it and start over, and who reminds me it's okay to take calculated creative risks at the last minute.

Just as my writer's block began to lift, my path finally crossed with that of the Orthodox School of Theology at Trinity College in Toronto, a program that was once a name on a website and is composed of people I'm now blessed to call colleagues. I would especially like to thank Richard Schneider, Daniel Opperwall, Fr. Theodore Paraskevopoulos, and Fr. Geoffrey Ready for their ongoing support and encouragement. In particular, it was Fr. Geoffrey's "timely" talk at the Resurrection of the Logos panel in March 2017 that reminded me why I had started this book and gave me the final push I needed to finish it once and for all.

Finally, I wish to thank three individuals who have been with me since the beginning of this project and who have given thorough feedback on the entire draft manuscript. First, to Melissa Naasko: I barely knew you before starting this book, but I am now blessed to call you my friend. Thank you for being generous with your time, reading energies, and words of affirmation. You continue to be more enthusiastic about my writing than I am, and I couldn't have done it without you.

To my spiritual father, Fr. Steven Kostoff: Who knew that girl you reprimanded for lounging around with her hands in her pockets her first time in your church would go on to write a book about spiritual lethargy? God certainly works in "mysterious" ways, to borrow a few of your superfluous scare quotes. Jokes aside, your pastoral guidance and fatherly concern over the years have been something I deeply cherish. Many ideas in this book are directly or indirectly indebted to the wisdom and insight you tirelessly pass on to your flock, which I consider myself blessed to be a part of, albeit from a distance. My heartfelt thanks go to you and Presbytera Deborah for all the conversations, films, dinners, and emails dripping with sarcasm we have shared since those first days I wandered into your parish.

Most of all, to my husband, Basil: No matter how much I wanted to chuck some of these chapters into the trash, you never hesitated to rescue and improve them—sharpening what needed sharpening, softening what needed softening, and convincing me my ideas were worth writing about in the first place. You're my partner in ~~crime~~ time, always thinking and curious about the same things I am and challenging me to go further. Thank you for your endless love, support, sacrifice, encouragement, Greek lessons, and ruthless editing when needed ("Enough with the laundry analogies, already!"). I am not the easiest person to give advice to, but more than anyone I know, you embody what it means to speak the truth in love—I consider the completion of this project a shared accomplishment.

Introduction

IT WAS A WARM AUTUMN MORNING IN ELEMENTARY school. During the middle of a math lesson, my teacher escorted me down the hall to the school guidance counselor, Mrs. D.

"She was crying at her desk. We were doing calendars," my teacher told Mrs. D. "She's upset about the time thing again—I just don't understand." With warm hands and an even warmer smile, Mrs. D ushered me into her room, a tiny nook that had once been a janitor's closet. Despite its dinginess and small size, the room was one of my favorite places in the whole school. Instead of windows, the wall was plastered with drawings, a patchwork quilt of crayon and construction paper. As we tucked ourselves into the child-sized table that the narrow walls could barely contain, Mrs. D scooted a box of crayons towards me.

"Let's color!" She said. This was her ritual, her invitation—to talk or be silent, but mostly to be myself, with all my worries and fears, no matter how silly they seemed.

"So, I'm already seven and a half years old," I began, after selecting a crayon. "Plus, my dad just turned forty! I'm getting too old. Time goes too fast, and I can't stop it."

Other children went to Mrs. D with seemingly weightier

matters: a family member going back to jail, their parents divorc-
ing, their sibling dying of cancer. I, on the other hand, agonized
about time, about days and months and years, and about how they
all seemed to be slipping through my tiny fingers. Fortunately,
Mrs. D was not one to minimize a precocious little girl's existential crises. She nodded as I spoke, as though we shared something
deep and significant in common. Perhaps she knew then what
would take me years to discern, that underneath it all, it was not
some calendar lesson that upset me. I was coming to terms with
something every human must face: mortality. Impermanence.

Although I had thought about death before, I was only just
beginning to realize this specter was not an abstraction that only
visited distant relatives and movie characters. It would happen to
my parents and my brothers, and someday to me. Just as troubling
was time itself—that silent thread connecting me to the eventual-
ity of death seemed to unravel at a pace I had never before taken
notice of. Plainly and simply, I had awoken to the reality that life
is short. This new thought haunted me with a panic-stricken loneliness I can still feel, deep in my bones, now a quarter-century
later. Each time I tried to face the reality of death was like peering
over the precipice of a quarry filled with deep, inky water. I was
desperate for Mrs. D to tell me I was mistaken, to assure me—as
adults were fond of doing—that it would make sense when I was
older, that death was just a misunderstanding. Yet, only one thing
she said remains in my memory, a remark with which she ended
nearly every conversation I had with her:

It's good to talk about these things.

These words blanketed our conversations with a vague sacredness, echoes of the benediction our Creator bestowed upon this

world in the beginning: *it is good*. Probably she said this to everyone who confided in her. But back then, nestled into her office amid crayons and artwork, it seemed she meant it particularly for me, that it was *especially* good to talk about death, to talk about time. It was good to talk about how perplexing it is to live and laugh and love knowing that nothing lasts.

This was the first time I recall actively struggling with what I now recognize to be despondency. In late antiquity, the preferred term for this was the Greek word *acedia* (ακηδία), which literally means a lack of care or concern. Early theologians thought of despondency as an absence of effort, particularly in the spiritual life—we exert ourselves for the things we care about, and when we don't care about anything, we remain passive and inactive. Despondency is alternatively described as a slackness of the soul. Like a belt that has stretched with time, the soul grows loose with apathy and ceases to hold us up. From this kernel of disregard sprout restlessness, rumination, anxiety, despair, sadness, and distractibility—the common, albeit morose, bedfellows of despondency.

I am reminded by Kathleen Norris, however, that behind the symptoms of despondency—behind even the stubborn apathy—is pain.[1] It is the pain of existing in a world that has become haunted by impermanence and marred by fragmentation. We cease caring once the act of caring wounds us or becomes too heavy a burden to bear. The restlessness, the rumination, the distraction—they crop up to fill the empty spaces within us where meaningful concern and effort once dwelled. Dorothy Sayers put it bluntly when she described despondency as "the sin that believes nothing, cares to know nothing, seeks to know nothing, loves nothing, hates

For most of my life, I had no word for that strange fusion of sadness, restlessness, and distraction that sprang up whenever the awareness of life's brevity became too overwhelming.

nothing, finds purpose in nothing [. . .] and remains alive because there is nothing for which it will die."[2] For most of my life, I had no word for that strange fusion of sadness, restlessness, and distraction that sprang up whenever the awareness of life's brevity became too overwhelming. In time, I found ways of numbing the quandary of mortality. The sting of death's reality dulled into mindless avoidance, a way of living that flits from one distraction or aimless worry to the next.

This book is for anyone whose faith, like mine, has ever been shipwrecked by the hallmarks of despondent thinking: apathy, distraction, and despair. It is a condition as old as the ancients, one that Christian ascetics of late antiquity addressed with sober familiarity. As prevalent as this spiritual condition was in the early days of monasticism, however, I suspect it is even more pervasive today. Countless visible and invisible forces in our culture collude to form the perfect recipe for despondency: we actively deny the reality of death on the one hand while seeking lives of immediacy, self-focus, and leisure on the other. Even if we wish to sidestep such mentalities, it is difficult to locate domains in which a simple and authentic Christian life can be lived. Despondency quickly steps in to fill the empty spaces that litter our post-industrial Western world. Although this book may not say much to alleviate this predicament, it promises to start a conversation, to "talk about these things" as Mrs. D would say, because it is in recovering our words for what has been lost that light can be spoken into darkness.

✠ ✠ ✠

THIS BOOK OFFERS A SERIES OF REFLECTIONS ON THE intertwined relationship of time and despondency. It is not a systematic, academic analysis of either, but a synthesis of historical wisdom, contemporary connections, and personal reflections to shed light on how time affects our experience of both despondency and healing. Despondency—in all its complexity and cunningness—arises from a relationship to time that has become broken. It amounts to no less than a perpetual attempt by the mind to flee from the present moment, to disregard the gift of God's presence at each juncture of time and space. The path to healing—paved and well trodden by steadfast souls who have gone before us—is one and the same as the path back to the present.

My interest in the topics of time and despondency goes at least as far back as that morning in Mrs. D's office. In addition to marking in my memory the start of a lifelong struggle with despondency, the realizations that brought me to Mrs. D's room also filled me with wonder toward time. Awe is the humble appreciation of mystery, and there are few phenomena in this world more mysterious than time. It is invisible, yet unstoppable; known and yet unfathomable; linear and yet cyclical; fast and yet slow; a burden and yet a blessing.

Mrs. D's encouragement "to talk about these things" must have remained with me,

༄

Despondency quickly steps in to fill the empty spaces that litter our post-industrial Western world.

༄

No longer merely the engine of change and decay, time in the Orthodox liturgical setting seemed to bear something of eternity.

beckoning me to keep communicating and articulating and listening, to keep plumbing the quarries of my own existence. I devoted years of graduate study to investigating perceptions of time in the context of religious history, gleaning the rich ways that past societies (particularly Reformation-era Germany) honored the spiritual ramifications of time's passing. Historical research opened my eyes to the potential for Christian faith—grounded in the temporal reality of the Incarnation—to transform our lived experiences of time in the here and now.

It was during my graduate studies I encountered the Orthodox Church. One of my first impressions of Orthodox Christianity (besides a jarring dose of culture shock) was that time flows differently here. Something mysterious happened when I entered the church for services: time became beautiful. No longer merely the engine of change and decay, time in the Orthodox liturgical setting seemed to bear something of eternity.

Along with complementing my temporal wonder, Orthodoxy introduced me to vibrant traditions that guide how faith is lived. I soon gained a spiritual father, Fr. Steven, who shepherded me in my struggle against despondency. Among the first items we discussed was the intense, aimless boredom that afflicts me during prayer, not to mention life in general. Fr. Steven was adamant: boredom is no excuse to shirk off prayer, the lifeblood of faith and relationship. Giving in to aimlessness by switching to a more enticing activity, he told me, only intensifies boredom over the course of our lives. Instead, he advised me to lean into the seeming monotony of life and prayer—to be as consistent in prayer as my broken human efforts allow, especially when I'm bored. Whether I felt happy or engaged while doing so was to some degree beside the point: what was most significant was simply showing up in the prayer corner. Day after day. After day.

This was something new. Until then, I had mostly sought ways to make prayer more spontaneous and "sincere." Because of this, I had never stopped and looked my despondency in the face before. I never had to—something more exciting was always there to divert my attention: the next idea, the next Bible study, the next person's prayer request. The seamlessness of Orthodox liturgy and its ascetic emphasis on prayer, however, left no place to run or hide. Perhaps for the first time, I saw my despondency for what it truly was: a condition that robbed my entire self—body, soul, and spirit—of the freedom to dwell with Christ in love.

Eventually, I came across the works of Evagrius and his keen observations of despondency. Although his writings concerned the struggles of fourth-century desert monks, perusing them felt like reading my own spiritual biography. I researched and read anything about despondency I could, soon discovering there was little in English that explored the topic thoroughly from a practical, pastoral perspective. (The notable exception to this is Gabriel Bunge's *Despondency: The Spiritual Teaching of Evagrius Ponticus on Acedia*,[3] which I have relied on heavily in writing this book.)

The relative lack of resources on despondency was troubling, especially since the more I observed its patterns in myself, the more I saw them all around me. Norris puts it beautifully and soberly when she says that despondency

is not a relic of the fourth century or a hang-up of some
weird Christian monks, but a force we ignore at our peril.
Whenever we focus on the foibles of celebrities to the detri-
ment of learning more about the real world—the emergence
of fundamentalist religious and nationalist movements, the
economic factors endangering our reefs and rainforests, the
social and ecological damage caused by factory farming—
acedia is at work. Whenever we run to escape it, acedia
is there, propelling us to the "next best thing," another
paradise to revel in and wantonly destroy. [...] Acedia has
come so far with us that it easily attaches to our hectic and
overburdened schedules. We appear to be anything but
slothful, yet that is exactly what we are, as we do more and
care less, and feel pressured to do still more.[4]

Our culture is a breeding ground for the chronic apathy of
despondency and the aimless, distractible restlessness that comes
with it. If Evagrius complained about *the movement of the sun*
being too much of a distraction for some monks, what would he
think of the fast-paced modern lifestyle? Or smartphones? Or
superabundant cute kitten videos on YouTube?

The theological and doxological traditions of Eastern Christianity offer our modern world a healing alternative to the broken aspects of despondency and human time perceptions. In this
book, I hope to communicate this long-established wisdom not
only to fellow Christians, but to all spiritual pilgrims hoping to
recover a more whole, integrated experience of this short life *sub
specie aeternitatis*—in light of eternity.

⊞ ⊞ ⊞

I HAVE DIVIDED THIS BOOK INTO THREE SECTIONS. The first lays the groundwork, rooting concepts of despondency (Chapter 1) and time (Chapter 2) within the theological traditions of Orthodox thought. Chapter 3 introduces the principal argument of this book, namely that despondency boils down to a rejection of the present moment, which is a gift from God. Chapter 4 expands on this to explain the physical, mental, and spiritual avenues by which we make this escape.

Building on this foundation, the second section of the book (Chapters 5 through 7) conveys practical methods of combating despondency, all of which center on restoring one's relationship with the present moment through both prayer and lifestyle choices.

Finally, the conclusion points to Christ as the substance of the present moment. His Resurrection—made possible through His Incarnation—fills the empty vessels of time. The ultimate antidote to despondency is heeding the call to "re-present" the Resurrection—the victory of life over death—on a continual basis: in our worship, in our lives, and in our world.

✠ ✠ ✠

I BEGAN WRITING ABOUT THIS TOPIC FOR MYSELF, AS A way to map out the tricky terrain of despondency. After several years, my writing and research gave way to a five-part podcast series that aired on Ancient Faith Radio during Great Lent 2016. I am grateful to the numerous listeners who wrote me during those months and who have continued to lend encouragement through the *Time Eternal* blog. Their kindness and enthusiasm continue to remind me of the life-giving truth of Mrs. D's words so many years ago. In writing, I have a chance both to speak and to be silent, to be myself and to make room for others, and to give voice to a struggle that is common to so many of us. It is not always easy to have these conversations, but it is good nonetheless: when we begin talking, we learn to combat demons rather than fear them. We learn to operate outside apathy and despair. We learn how to start being—with ourselves, with one another, and slowly, with God. Writing this book has been an exercise in facing my demon(s). I pray it invites others to do the same, not merely as isolated individuals but as co-suffering members of the Body of Christ.

It's good to talk about these things.

PART I

REJECTING
THE PRESENT

Despondency, Time, and the Soul

CHAPTER 1

What Is Despondency?

*Despondency is the impossibility to see anything good or
positive; it is the reduction of everything to negativism and
pessimism. [. . .] Despondency is the suicide of the soul
because when man is possessed by it, he is absolutely unable
to see the light and desire it.*

—ALEXANDER SCHMEMANN[5]

*Under His wings you shall hope;
His truth shall encircle you with a shield.
You shall not be frightened by fear at night,
Nor from an arrow that flies by day,
Nor by a thing moving in darkness,
Nor by a mishap and a demon of noonday.*

(PS. 90/91:4–6)

RESTLESSNESS, RUMINATION, TORPOR, SLOTH, distractibility, disinterest, despair—these are the symptoms of a
ruthless interior sickness whose spiritual ramifications were first
described by Evagrius Ponticus (d. AD 399), a humble ascetic
father deep in the Nitrian Desert of Egypt. Writing to help his fellow monastics, Evagrius observed that some monks were unable
to endure solitude—not to mention prayer, labor, or other quotidian tasks—for any sustained duration. He would find them

outside their cells, visiting others or staring listlessly at the sun. They disdained their surroundings and any tasks placed before them. As Evagrius monitored these monks, he came to realize they suffered from a crippling inward condition that gradually drained all vitality from their lives. In their ennui, monks sought to escape through excessive sleep, socializing, or aimless reading. Yet even these pastimes quickly lost their appeal, pushing the monks further into their desperate, anxious idleness.

Evagrius gave the beast a name: acedia (ακηδία). In English, I use the term despondency—it evokes, for me, the sticky web of sadness and rumination, the "strange laziness and passivity of our entire being which always pushes us 'down' rather than 'up.'"[6] The apathy of despondency is not to be confused with *apatheia*, the condition of being untethered to passions and demons, which the Fathers praised. In despondency, we fail to care about things that should actually matter to us, such as cultivating a life of spiritual effort or seeking the well-being of our neighbor. Once apathy infects one corner of our lives, it quickly metastasizes elsewhere. As soon as we start neglecting prayer, we find it easier to disregard our chores, or our children, or the homeless man on the street.

Beneath the many symptoms, Evagrius believed despondency arises from desire and anger—anger toward what is present, desire for what is not.[7] Out of this two-pronged dissatisfaction comes a lack of care, a total apathy and indifference. Yet I think we could also say that there is something more primary than desire and anger at stake: pain. Anger is a covering for our pain; we stop caring when we are wounded by the laceration of existence—whether that comes in the form of sadness, fear, disappointment, or shame. The human condition—the condition of bearing the image of God in a world of brokenness—could be summed up as learning to live (and love) in the midst of pain, learning to dwell where there is shame, toil, and adversity.

Such a way of being does not come naturally; we instinctively minimize hurt and conceal our shame. The first thing Adam and Eve did after eating of the tree of knowledge of good and evil was to cover themselves. This tendency to avoid the reality of pain has filtered down even to the muscular and molecular level—our bodies readily sink into poor posture to sidestep the sting of sitting up straight, and over time our muscles grow weak and loose from ill use. Such is the case in our souls, too—when our minds abandon the pain of caring, our spiritual tendons grow slack. We lose the capacity to focus, behold, encounter, and love, which likewise provokes a toxic kind of emptiness—a vacuum that attracts all manner of distraction, restlessness, rumination, anxiety, fear, and lethargy.

For many of us, despondency is the oldest and most pernicious spiritual struggle of our lives. Looking back on my own experiences, my first and faintest memories of despondency predate those of praying. There is a real possibility that for some, despondency is a more or less congenital condition, shaping our spiritual perceptions almost from birth. Perhaps that's why turning away from it can feel a lot like dying—it *is* a death (albeit a slow and gradual one), a surrendering of perhaps the only way we have ever perceived the world. But this death is also the way of new life.

My understanding of despondency is indebted to Evagrius's centuries-old reflections, which lend perennial insight into this "unnatural slackness of the soul."[8] His interest in the topic was not merely intellectual but personal. He actively endured his own bouts of despondency and, as a spiritual father, shepherded others out of the depths of despair with the desire to help "make the human being capable of loving again, and thereby capable of God."[9] Countless beloved theologians of the Orthodox tradition have embroidered upon his insights, among them Ss. John Cassian, Gregory, John Climacus, John of Damascus, and John of Kronstadt. Like Evagrius, they saw despondency as a monastic concern, yet their wisdom is relevant to anyone for whom apathy, boredom, restlessness, and distraction have become hurdles to spiritual growth.

Despondency has an infinite array of disguises and symptoms. Among the most universal signs is inner restlessness, yet this can present itself in countless ways, depending on the person. For some, the restlessness makes it problematic to sit alone, to read a book to completion, to pray for any length or intensity, or to finish a task at work. Others can perform all of these activities but find themselves hounded by a stubborn anger or boredom while doing so. For still others, despondency begins as an inclination toward sleep, eating, distraction, or worry. Many of the most prominent faces of despondency are captured in this short verse:

> Despondency:
>   breezy love,
> tramper of steps,
>   hater of love of work,
> fight against solitude,
>   thunderstorm of psalmody,
> aversion to prayer,
>   slackening of asceticism [spiritual effort],

ill-timed slumber,
    sleep, tossing and turning,
burden of solitude,
    hatred of the cell,
adversary of ascetical efforts,
    counter-attacking against endurance,
impediment to reflection,
    ignorance of the Scriptures,
companion of sadness,
    daily rhythm of hunger.[10]

Despondents tend to cover a lot of ground, wandering hither and thither through the mundanities of life without ever finishing or accomplishing anything in particular. And when that doesn't work, we manipulate even necessary activities like sleeping and eating—normally peaceful and life-giving—to serve our apathy. They become desperate efforts to soak up the boredom leaking out of every orifice of life.

Who has not wrestled with the temptation of inattention or distraction in daily life? Who has not faced tedium in prayer? At some point, we all contend with this in one way or another. And when these momentary struggles are not addressed quickly—and sometimes even when they are—apathy, rumination, and despair become semi-permanent afflictions. This can have tragic consequences: despondency is ultimately the most destructive spiritual struggle and gradually threatens "to suffocate [. . .] the core of the human being."[11] To get a better sense of how despondency does its damage, it is helpful to explore the inward topography of the human person—mind, heart, and soul—through the lens of Eastern Orthodox thought.

DESPONDENCY & THE SOUL

Despondency is first and foremost an ailment of the soul, that is, the spiritual core of an individual. In Scripture, this aspect of personhood is commonly referred to as the heart:

> If the heart of man is controlled by feelings, his soul is sorrowful. (Prov. 14:10)

> Prove me, O Lord, and test me, / Try my reins and my heart in the fire. (Ps. 25/26:2)

Another term for the heart or soul is the *nous* (νοῦς), from which the English term *noetic* derives. Technically speaking, Orthodox theologians understand the soul to consist of two parallel energies. On the one hand is the rationalizing function of the soul, which expresses itself by measuring, reasoning, judging, and categorizing.[12] In my writing, the *mind* (and the adjectives *mental* and *intellectual*) refers to this faculty. By contrast, the terms *heart* and *nous*, used interchangeably, are reserved for the heart, that quieter, more receptive energy of the soul that Ss. Theophan the Recluse and Dimitry of Rostov spoke of as the inner prayer chamber.[13] Likewise, the *soul*—in this book, at least—consists of both mind and heart.

Like the body, the soul can become sick, particularly when the mind dominates the heart. Despondency is one of many intrusive thoughts (*logismoi*, λογισμοί) of the mind that can oppress and afflict the nous, much like an illness. Although the best translation of *logismoi* into English is "thoughts," the word refers not just to the simple deductions and calculations the mind must make in the course of everyday life—deciding what items to write on a grocery list (although this does require thought) is probably not a logismos in the spiritual sense. If, on the other hand, the shopping list invites distracting fantasies about a decadent meal we might prepare with the ingredients on that list—and in our zeal to go home and cook, we consider trampling down those ahead of us in the checkout line—then we are probably getting closer to the realm of logismoi. Such intrusive thoughts consist of imaginative representations rather than simple responses to daily necessities.

Not all logismoi are necessarily "bad" or negative, but all carry the potential to cause problems if we cling too tightly to them. For example, paying too much attention to a kind compliment can gradually lead to self-inflation. Like an unsolicited artist, logismoi paint on the canvas of our minds images of the world that may or may not be based in reality.[14] Logismoi begin relatively harmlessly, as a "flowing river" of quiet imaginings that rushes softly past. If we heed them, however, they eventually transform into a deluge from which the heart cannot escape.[15]

Evagrius viewed despondency as one of a handful of dominant logismoi that he termed the "eight evil thoughts." His enumeration was among the earliest catalogues of destructive thought and sin patterns in the Christian tradition. Alongside despondency, he recognized anger, gluttony, vainglory, lust, greed, sadness, and pride. By the late fifth century, particularly in the writings of St. Gregory I, these eight thoughts were consolidated into seven, in part by combining despondency (acedia) and sadness (*tristitia*) into a composite, usually referred to in English as *sloth*.[16]

These so-called seven deadly sins became a popular framework for categorizing sin in the medieval West for centuries. This and similar models, however, failed to flourish in the Eastern realm of Christianity. To draw too firm a boundary between individual sins (or even between sinning and not sinning) misses the point: sin is an indication of brokenness, which extends in all directions, not just through an individual but through the entire creation. Rather than a multitude of isolated transgressions, sin in Orthodox thought is more like an overarching sickness, a single web with countless invisible threads that ensnare us individually and collectively.

Even Evagrius's eight logismoi were intended only as a starting point, a heuristic tool to help us begin recognizing thought patterns that lead to sin. Similar groupings have been devised by other Orthodox theologians over the centuries—one thinks, for example, of St. Thessalios's three basic thoughts (gluttony, self-esteem or pride, and avarice).[17] None of these catalogues, however, has been followed with dogmatic or canonical faithfulness, nor have they witnessed the cultural and ecclesiastical popularity the seven deadly sins enjoyed in Western Europe. In reality, there are probably many more than three, seven, or eight pathways to sin. But such lists aid our recognition of the most archetypal snares that litter the path of salvation.

An equally significant clarification in regard to these lists involves the term *sin* itself, which may give the wrong impression to a post-modern Western audience, for whom the term carries vastly different associations than it would have had in pre-medieval Christendom. Like most of his peers, Evagrius did not view the various logismoi as punishable transgressions, but instead as destructive modes of being—destructive to ourselves, first of all, but also to those around us. "Sin," wrote Fr. Alexander

Schmemann, "is always absence of love, and therefore separation, isolation, war of all against all. The new life given by Christ [. . .] is, first of all, a life of reconciliation, of 'gathering into oneness those who were dispersed,' the restoration of love broken by sin."[18]

According to Orthodox concepts of this brokenness, even the most harmful thoughts only become sins when we freely cooperate with them by nourishing them in our minds and acting on them. There is not always a clear-cut line between these phases, and to try to draw one would miss the point. Even after a thought has become sin, it is merely a symptom of an interior brokenness in need of healing, not a legal transgression to be punished as soon as we break the law. When not addressed quickly, the thoughts we collaborate with slowly poison the whole person, and in this sense can be quite "deadly." Indeed, even in the West during the Middle Ages, the seven deadly sins were sometimes described not as sins (*peccatorum*) but rather as vices (*vitia*), a word that I think speaks to the stubborn and long-lasting nature of destructive habits.[19]

The close conceptual relationship between thought, sin, and spiritual sickness requires deeper analysis, particularly in the case of despondency, which so closely resembles one of the more heartbreaking afflictions of our times: clinical depression. Has the Church, now or in the past, considered depression a sin?

DESPONDENCY & DEPRESSION

I have personally witnessed the tragedy that can occur when people assume clinical depression is a sin or the direct result thereof. I have watched some try to pray away mental health issues, attempting to combat depression by conjuring up more hope or faith or discipline. I have watched others grow dejected over the lack of sensitivity toward mental health they encountered in Christian circles and leave the faith altogether. These misrepresentations and misunderstandings are hardly trivial and warrant a deeper, nuanced discussion.

In taking on this subject, I should disclose that my mode of analysis is historical and conceptual rather than medical—I was trained as a historian, not a mental health professional. By virtue of my background, though, I am aware that as the Church, we have historically neglected to speak clearly, consistently, and redemptively to mental and emotional suffering. As a sad but perhaps logical consequence, mainstream Western culture is largely suspicious of Christian attitudes toward mental health issues. An expression of this can be found in Andrew Solomon's best-selling book on depression, whose title borrows Evagrius's moniker for despondency ("the noonday demon"). At one point, Solomon argues that despondency (acedia) was the medieval Church's equivalent term for what we now call depression. As Solomon sees it, Christianity's tendency to attribute despondency/depression to sin is partly responsible for today's stigmatization of mental health issues.[20]

Though this reading of historical theology fails to consider the nuances of early Christian understandings, I believe Solomon—who does not pretend to be a Christian or a theologian—does the Church a favor by clearly elucidating a message Christianity has failed to communicate to the wider culture, past and present. Even in Orthodox circles, which tend to be a bit more conversant with distant historical theology than other corners of modern Christianity, one finds ample evidence of the conflation of depression and sin.[21] This is something we must be more vigilant about in twenty-first–century Christianity. When we equate historical spiritual concepts with modern diagnoses, we blur the lines between spiritual ill health, moral culpability, and medical necessity. We risk cheapening and deadening the contributions both theology and medicine have to make to the healing of brokenness.

Leaving aside the discussion of sin for a moment, let us address depression and despondency in greater detail. To be sure, these conditions share much in common, so much so that they can be difficult to distinguish or clearly diagnose. Like two circles of a Venn diagram, they overlap on many of their symptoms—irritability, fatigue, restlessness, boredom, and hopelessness are just some examples. Nonetheless, despondency and depression are separate circles; the two concepts have entirely different historical roots and are associated with divergent paradigms concerning the human person.

Our knowledge of depression is rooted in the body-centered perceptions of Western medicine, which sees this affliction through the lens of physical processes like biochemical imbalances or weakened mood regulators in the brain. Concepts of despondency, on the other hand, originated in the soul-centered worldview of early Christian monasticism. That is not to say despondency has no physical manifestations, but simply that it begins in the soul and works outward to poison and paralyze the entire human person.

Taking these paradigms into account is a vital step in understanding—and being healed of—despondency. I don't believe the different understandings of despondency and depression boil down to scientific advancement, but rather that Evagrius's and the

Fathers' soul-centered view of human personhood has value in its own right. Think of the long shift from Ptolemy's Earth-centered solar system to the heliocentric cosmographies of Copernicus and Galileo. Both models contained the same items—the sun, moon, planets, and stars. Depending on what occupied the center of the cosmos, however, the relationships between these objects took on divergent meanings. The point is not to pit Western medicine against early Christian theology (or vice versa)—both have a role to play in helping humanity. But if we wish to understand despondency, we have to evaluate it on its own terms and in its own context, not through the lens of modern medicine.

For early Christian monastics, despondency was seen as an ailment of the soul that spread to the body and beyond. Whenever the soul becomes ill, writes Metropolitan Hierotheos of Nafpaktos, "instead of being nourished by God, [it] sucks the body dry."[22] As far back as the fourth century, Evagrius mentioned a host of physical manifestations of despondency that included bodily weakness and excessive sleep. Considering the outward destruction despondency can cause, Evagrius described it as the worst of the logismoi—when left unchecked, he noted, it can lead to suicide.[23]

To make matters worse, the poison of spiritual sickness does not stop at the individual level. The tendrils of the web of sin spread outward to "the body, society and the entire creation."[24] Yet just as the poison of spiritual sickness begins in the soul, so too does healing. Even after despondency has affected the body or those around us, restoration starts within us and unfolds in new directions to revive all aspects of a person's self and life. We could even extend this healing further, to entire societies and ecosystems. In other words, the restoration of a single human soul has almost limitless transformative effects that ripple throughout the rest of the world.

DESPONDENCY & "SIN"

Having discussed the relationship between despondency and depression, we return to the question of sin. Just like a sickness, sin has a certain course, a certain way it progresses. Despondency (like all sins) begins as a harmful, intrusive mode of thinking. With that point, at least, it is hard to take issue—no one welcomes inner agitation, continual apathy, or chronic boredom. Such modes of being degrade rather than benefit one's quality of life.

Despondency does not stop at sporadic thoughts, though. It rages on, eventually dominating the whole shape of the mind. Evagrius observed, for example, that it impels people to engage in increasingly self-destructive mental habits—the more we ruminate, the more the mind cannot help ruminating. After a while, thoughts solidify into a passion, a more firmly established (if skewed) reality within the human person.

Despondency is a sickness in need of healing rather than a crime in need of punishment.

Finally, despondency (like all passions) tempts individuals to move past mere thought until they give their assent, eventually acting on the destructive undercurrents of the mind. The thought may occur to a recovering alcoholic to have a drink, for example, but in merely having that thought he has done nothing harmful—we cannot control our thoughts any more than we can control how much it rains. However, if he acts on that thought by actually taking a drink, he is definitely off the bandwagon. "Consent," also called "cooperation," is the gray area between thought and action—at some point, the recovering alcoholic inwardly said "yes" to the prospect of having a drink. It is at that juncture when sin begins to take root within us, because once we give our consent to a thought, it is almost inevitable we will eventually act on it.

Action, by the way, is not always (or even usually) overtly physical or visible—you can throw a stone in anger, but you can also be a stone wall of silence for the same reason. There are sins of omission and commission, and many of the outward "actions" of despondency consist of the apathetic failure to act when action is not only warranted but would be helpful to our condition. We adopt procrastination as a sort of existential mandate, putting off responsibilities and tasks until we feel like doing them.

As soon as a person commits an action in service of a passion—in other words, sins—he or she becomes even more entangled with it. A thousand years before neuroscientists discovered the reward system of the brain, the Church knew that actions and behaviors create within us pleasurable connections that become increasingly difficult to redirect.[25] Sin begets entrenched habits of sin, and the pattern continues. Soon, we find ourselves enslaved to a mode of living entirely shaped by what once began as an innocuous, fleeting thought. The tragedy, here, is not that sin angers God, but that it erodes our capacity to choose Him at all. At a certain point, it begins to feel as though we have no agency left. As much as we hate what it does to us, we cannot *not* be despondent.

In this way, the "sin" of despondency behaves much more like a sickness in need of healing than a crime in need of punishment—a distinction that forms the basis for Orthodox concepts of sin and salvation.[26] Like any illness, sin has a particular course and progression as it develops. If we were to compare sin to cancer, a logismos would be akin to a pre-cancerous growth—not cancer (yet), but necessary to monitor and deal with sooner rather than later. To stretch the analogy further, cancer is often discovered only after it causes physical symptoms. Similarly, the actions we eventually commit when guided by our logismoi are merely the external symptoms of a much deeper problem.

∿

Sin is fragmentation— between ourselves and our neighbor, between ourselves and God, and also between the very parts that constitute our selves.

∿

That problem is fragmentation—between ourselves and our neighbor, between ourselves and God, and also between the very parts that constitute our selves. We inherit this fragmented existence from those who came before us, just as we inherit genes and illnesses. Separating us from wholeness and intactness, sin shatters us. It divorces us not only from God but also from our true desires and potentiality, particularly our capacity to act freely as His creatures. It is when this capacity is lost or begins to be lost that sin becomes most damaging. This is not an intellectual judgment but an experiential reality that anyone who has ever struggled with a profound sense of despondency can relate to— the mentality becomes like an inner prison, its walls becoming progressively narrower despite our best efforts.

If sin is spiritual sickness, the place of healing is the Church. Here, we find reintegration: with Christ, who is the Head of the Church, and with our neighbor. The sacraments of confession, healing, and the Eucharist reunite us to God and to the reality of ourselves, both soul and body. We are surrounded, too, by prayers that seek unity and peace for all believers and for the whole world. Just as the sinews of sin stretch out in all directions, so too does prayer in the Church, mystically restoring and recovering what has been lost. In the Church, we are awakened out of our stupor. In other words, the Church is (or should be) a hospital, not a courtroom:

> Sin takes us away from communion, to what might be called
> disunion, with God and neighbor. St. John Chrysostom
> states: "Did you commit sin? Enter the Church [. . .] for
> here is the physician, not the judge; here one is not inves-
> tigated, one receives remission of sins" [. . .] If the Church
> is a "physician," then Her role is to heal the break with God
> and neighbor. Sin is missing the mark of being centered
> on God and His Will and is considered, therefore, to be an
> illness or infirmity. With healing we are restored to a former
> condition.[27]

To sum things up, the Church has historically seen despondency as one of many indications that a person is unwell, a symptom of a brokenness that can fragment and distort all levels of our experience.

DESPONDENCY & TIME

Despondency is the most temporal of the spiritual passions. It is the only one associated with a particular time of day—references to the "noonday demon" are at least as old as the Psalms (see 90/91:6). Evagrius observed that this passion most frequently attacks from about the fourth hour (10 am) until the ninth hour

(2 pm).[28] Midday was not the only time when despondency could strike, but for Evagrius, it seemed to be the most common one. He spent much of his monastic tenure deep in the deserts of Egypt—not a pleasant place to be when the sun is hovering around its zenith. Evagrius saw that many monks whiled away the long hours of the day by sleeping and sitting around, hardly the ascetic behavior monasticism strives for. In tandem with this outward laziness, Evagrius found that the heat of midday encouraged a lax consciousness that resulted in either mental exhaustion or frenetic agitation.

On a deeper level, the middle of the day represents what I call the penultimate moments of life, the times we are almost but not quite finished, so close and yet so far. By the time we make it to the heat of the afternoon, we've already made it out of bed and through the rigors of the morning. We've come so far, yet it seems like a sweltering eternity stands between us and the cool of evening. Psychologically, this tension is extremely hard to withstand and often gives way to frantic, desperate attempts to speed things along. The Israelites made it out of Egypt, through the Red Sea, and into the desert that would take them to the promised land. Yet just before God could make good on His promise, they resorted to idolatry. It was a "midday" moment—they'd come so far, and suddenly things slowed to a standstill. In their despondency, they fled from God and into a new, self-fashioned reality.

The propensity for despondency to strike in the middle of the day is not the only way this spiritual sickness infects our sense of time. In a wider sense, despondency epitomizes how sin and brokenness feeds and is fed by a fragmented, antagonistic relationship to temporality. Much more remains to be said concerning the relationship between time and despondency. First, though, it is helpful to step back and examine more broadly what time is and the purpose it serves in creation.

CHAPTER 2

Time and Despondency

Does anyone ever realize life while they live it—every, every minute?

—EMILY IN *OUR TOWN* BY THORNTON WILDER

Whatever happens,
those who have learned
to love one another
have made their way
into the lasting world.

—WENDELL BERRY, *SABBATHS* (1998) I[29]

Glory to Thee, who cure affliction and emptiness with the healing flow of time.

—AKATHIST OF THANKSGIVING, IKOS 8

Our Town, A PLAY WRITTEN BY THORNTON WILDER IN 1938, follows a simple, Depression-era town and the ordinary relationships that unfold there. At the center of the story are George and Emily, who grow up together and eventually marry. The last act of the drama takes place in the cemetery of the town, where the audience learns who has died in the nine years since their wedding. Sadly, Emily herself is among them, having passed away in childbirth.

In Wilder's rendition of the afterlife, the dead can talk and observe life as it goes on without them but cannot interact with the living in any meaningful way. The dead spend most of their time sitting alone on hard chairs, their faces gazing into the void of a darkened theater—ever seeing, but never truly living. They can relive moments from their past lives, but only as invisible spectators unable to communicate with those they love.

Despite warnings from other members of the cemetery, Emily returns to an ordinary day from her life, the morning of her twelfth birthday. She sees with new eyes the beauty of even mundane interactions with her family and the care her mother bestowed on all the little details of everyday life. Ultimately, the memory proves too painful for Emily—it confronts her with the magnitude of all she took for granted. In tears, she returns to her isolated cemetery existence with a line that has haunted me since I first saw the play performed in high school: "Does anyone ever realize life while they live it—every, every minute?"

What grieved Emily was her failure to see life for what it was in time. Her lament expresses the crux of the human condition and the painful regret that often undergirds despondency. How difficult it is to recognize the everyday beauty of each moment before life ushers us onward.

Perceiving this grim reality, the ancients blamed time—or at least the change, decay, and mortality it brings about. Plato, for example, believed eternity was essentially different from time—not just *longer* than time, but utterly time-*less*, devoid of time.[30] And because time stood for change and decay, it was deemed inferior to eternity, which was immutable and perfect.

The vestiges of Plato's worldview still resonate with most of us two and a half millennia later. In our Western world, too, time and eternity are regarded as separate, even dichotomous entities. Time is here and all around us, while eternity is somewhere upwards or out there—if it exists at all, we will find out only after we have died in this life of time. Summing up the dominant view of our age, historian Carlos Eire inquires:

> [W]hat might eternity be? Is it anything other than a purely abstract concept, totally unrelated to our lives or worse, a frightfully uncertain horizon, best summed by Vladimir Nabokov: "The cradle rocks above an abyss, and our common sense tells us that our existence is but a brief crack of light between two eternities of darkness"?[31]

What's at stake in such a division is our entire way of being in the world, particularly as Christians. For one thing, prayer seems rather pointless if time is so antithetical to an eternal God. Does a cosmic bubble quote hover above the present moment, feeding our words and prayers to the "big guy upstairs" so He needn't sully Himself by dwelling among us? Speaking of dwelling among us—there's the whole Incarnation to reconsider. If time and eternity are truly separate realms—that is, if God is strictly eternal and we are strictly temporal—then Christ could not have come in the flesh. And without the Incarnation, there can be no resurrection, no salvation, no real interaction between the world of flesh and spirit. If that were truly the case, despondency would seem the sane, healthy response. What reason is there to hope if, to restate Nabokov's chilling words, "our existence is but a brief crack of light between two eternities of darkness"?

Yet what if time and eternity are not as diametrically opposed as they seem to be? Indeed, such a dichotomy was largely foreign to early Christians, who (like their ancient Jewish ancestors) viewed time as a divine extension of eternity. Both were thought to be made of the same *stuff*; eternity is just made with infinitely more of it. Whereas time on earth consists of a limited number of ages or eons, eternity was seen as an endless number of ages that unfolds simultaneously with time, but which also extends beyond the temporal parameters of this world.[32] Although early Christians inherited this harmonized cosmology from Judaism, their belief in Christ's Incarnation—the entrance of God's Son into our world of time and flesh—bolstered the sense that time and eternity were somehow fused.

Whispers of this ancient Christian cosmology can still be heard in various denominational traditions, but it has been acutely preserved in the Christian East. Here, time has never been regarded as a cold or distant force, but as a direct extension (*diastema*) of eternity that serves to reveal the love of God through His Son. To put it another way, time is the dimensional fabric that allows relationship and action to happen. Without it, there would be little prospect of communion, forgiveness, or change of heart—all life-giving possibilities hinge on the interaction of time and eternity in the here and now of our existence. When we begin to look at these two realms from the vantage point of Christ and human relationship, it seems that eternity is not as far off as we often assume.

In fact, eternal life—and with it, healing from despondency—begins when we start to exercise that capacity to "realize" life while we live it: every, every minute, as Emily so eloquently put it. This chapter seeks to recover this sense of unity between time and eternity, particularly as it relates to the process of healing from despondency.

TIME AND ETERNITY: A CHRISTOLOGICAL VIEW

The worldview of the Christian East centers on a radical and incarnational sense of synergy between time and eternity—both reveal important aspects of God's nature. Eternity manifests God as being; time manifests Him as action. In this framework, God is not eternal per se—He *is* eternity, the source from which all eternity flows. Something similar could be said of time—God is neither temporal nor atemporal, but rather the essence of time, the life-giving form and content of it.

How can both time and eternity flow from the same God? Drawing on the Cappadocian fathers and St. John of Scythopolis, professor of philosophy David Bradshaw likens God's time-eternal unity to a kiss given by a husband to his wife.[33] For a husband to simply *be* in love with his wife is not enough—to manifest or communicate that love to her (to make his love experientially real to his wife) he must *act,* for example by kissing her. It is only through action that a wife understands the love of her husband. In this example, love and the kiss are part of the same package—it would make little sense to speak of the kiss as opposed to or even separate from the husband's love. Indeed, the single kiss comes from the husband's more perennial, continuous state of love toward his wife. Yet without a kiss—or some other act— his love would have no real meaning, since it

∾

In eternity, we understand God as being, whereas in time, we understand Him as action.

∾

would not be communicated or shared with his wife. In other words, the being and acting modes of love are mutually reinforcing, integrally connected aspects of what it means to love.

If we compare this example to the relationship between time and eternity, it seems that temporality was not an accidental byproduct of creation but rather an organic extension of God-in-action. The first words of the Judeo-Christian creation narrative—really, of the entire Bible—are a temporal marker: "In the beginning." The entirety of God's message to man flows from that beginning—the beginning of time, yes, but that is simply another way of saying the beginning of when love became manifested as action. Out of that action, creation was born.

Whether one interprets the six days of Genesis as literal or typological intervals (the Church Fathers favored the latter), the narrative arc of creation is inherently temporal. It is rooted in sequence—a first, next, and last, with one creative act layered upon the next. The luminaries were ushered into being ahead of breathing creatures and given the vocation of marking time (Gen. 1:14, 15), thus manifesting temporality in visible signs. The last layer of creation was unfurled when God, resting from His labors, "blessed the seventh day and sanctified it" (Gen. 2:3). This final day of creation is a proxy not just for all subsequent Sabbaths, but for all of time on earth—the way it goes forth yet returns, always, to rest in the peace of eternity. When reading this narrative, it is difficult to see the baseness of time Plato and others lamented—in these first few scenes of Genesis, change is holy. Each new development brought about more life and beauty than before—making God's love more manifest and capable of being encountered. Likewise, each addition to creation was beheld and blessed by its Maker before He moved to the next.

However, when the sickness of sin entered the world shortly thereafter, our experience of time was shattered, bifurcated. Now, time did not allow only for life but also for death: "In toil you shall eat from [the ground] all the days of your life. Both thorns and thistles it shall bring forth for you [. . .] till you return to the ground from which you were taken. Earth you are, and to earth you shall return" (Gen. 3:17–19). Whereas once, time manifested the ever-new bounties of God's creative goodness, after the Fall it was marred by death—no matter how hard we toil or hope, we will one day die.

It is the apparent futility of living and dying that, more than any other factor, invites the apathy of despondency. Since we cannot exceed the temporal bounds God has set for our lives (Job 14:5), why bother with anything? In his novel *The Dying Animal,* Philip Roth wrote, "In every calm and reasonable person there is a hidden second person scared witless about death." Even for Christ, the conquering of death was a hard-earned battle, full of literal blood, sweat, and tears—the joy of the Resurrection by no means minimizes the grief that death and separation inflicted through the Cross.

It is here in the face of death that time seems most imprisoning, a slave-master that tethers us to the present, to aging, and ultimately to our death. But traditionally, the slow descent of our lives was interpreted not as a punishment but as a mercy. When Adam and Eve exercised their free will by cutting themselves off from God, they alienated the source of life. The result should have been death, immediate and all-encompassing. Instead, however, God paved a new path for us. He clothed the nakedness of His

creatures not only with animal skins (3:21), but also with the
promise of time itself—the slow pace of decay over the course of
a lifespan:

> After Adam's sin, God, through His great love and com-
> passion, clothed man in garments of skin. In the teaching
> of the Holy Fathers we see that these garments of skin are
> the decay and mortality which entered man's body after sin.
> The decay connsists [sic] of the illnesses, weaknesses and
> hardships of human life, how man is conceived, is carried
> in the womb, is born, and finally journeys towards death. In
> reality the whole life of man is a series of successive deaths,
> it is a lingering death.[34]

Why would God subject His creatures to this slow, "lingering"
death—would it not have been more loving to put us out of our
misery? To appreciate the love behind such a gesture, we have
to recall what it is that time affords us: the opportunity to turn
toward (or away from) God, life, love, and goodness. Like a lover
or a friend, God left space for a path back to relationship. In the
fullness of time, Christ entered our world to pave this path for
our sake. His Incarnation and Resurrection open the door for
us, as God's creatures, to "redeem time," to use the oft-spoken
phrase of St. Paul in his epistles (see Eph. 5:16; Col. 4:5). This is
the starting point for an Orthodox theology of time: though our
relationship to time has been fractured by sin, we can recover the
inherent goodness of time through encountering the love of God
as revealed in His Son.

Expanding on this foundation, we could say that all moments
in time are potential vessels of eternity. In biblical terms, the

durational, chronological current of time is known as *chronos*. Chronos is the tick and tock of the clock, the ebb and flow of months and years. It's what time does when left to its own devices. *Kairos* time, on the other hand, consists of interruptions in chronos, junctures at which God acts in time (or when we act in eternity, a thought we will revisit in the next section). Metropolitan Kallistos Ware says that kairos is "characterized not by the predeter-

> ∽
>
> *The God of the Bible is not opposed to time, but is actively working in and through it to communicate His love to His creatures.*
>
> ∽

mined swing of the pendulum but by unpredictable yet decisive moments of opportunity, moments of disclosure filled with meaning when clock time stands still, when eternity breaks in."[35] Kairos moments remind us that the God of the Bible is not morally opposed to time but in fact is intimately and actively working in and through it to communicate His love to His creatures.

We can all look back on our lives and recall our own kairos moments, junctures at which "God breaks through to us, or when we break through to God," to borrow a phrase from Metropolitan Anthony (Bloom) of Sorouzh.[36] As quietly and briefly as these moments pass by, they cause our souls to resound with the words of Jacob: "The LORD is in this place and I did not know *it*" (Gen. 28:16). Then there are the more global kairos moments, the pivotal junctures in salvific history, first and foremost the Incarnation and the Resurrection of Christ. These are the temporal bookends of the resurrection of created time. In entering our world of flesh and death, Christ sanctified time—He affirmed its capacity to bear eternity, just as Mary bore Christ in her womb. Then, rising again, He disentangled time from its inexorable relationship with death. Because death no longer has the final word on existence, time was restored to its former glory, filled with divine presence. St. Athanasius put it beautifully when he wrote:

> The Self-revealing of the Word is in every dimension—
> above, in creation; below, in the Incarnation; in the depth,
> in Hades; in the breadth, throughout the world. All things
> have been filled with the knowledge of God.[37]

The kairos events of Christ's life are not hypothetical, philosophical ideals to be tucked away in dusty tomes—they change everything. Or, perhaps more accurately, they *can* change everything—if we are willing.

Like the being and act of love, "[t]ime and eternity are not opposed but interdependent, not mutually exclusive but complementary."[38] From this vantage point, time is the dimension in which action(s) play out unceasingly and eternally. In all its moments and durations, time (chronos) is meant to become kairotic; it is meant to bear God's movement toward us and our movement toward Him—we do not have to wait until time is over to taste eternity.

TIME AND ETERNITY: A RELATIONAL VIEW

So how do we experience eternity? The short answer is, in relationship. If time is eternal love in action, we partake of eternity when we somehow participate in that love, whether by turning toward Christ or toward our fellow man. Recalling Emily's lament in the last act of *Our Town*, her grief was not that she had overlooked life generally, but that she had overlooked the particularity of love, the "every, every minute" of encountering and responding to relationship.

The longer answer is: through the Trinity. The community shared within the Triune God is the prototype of all relationship. In his essay "Eternity and Time," the late Fr. Dumitru Staniloae reasoned that at the heart of the Trinity is love, which we could define as "the gift of oneself to another, and [. . .] the full return of that gift from the other in response."[39] In other words, love is a closed loop—it consists not just of the initial act or expression of love *to* the recipient, but also the recipient's response to that act of love. Unlike human relationships, within the Trinity there is no delay between this

> *Time is the medium or interface that makes it possible to act in and respond to love.*

giving and responding—the gift of one Person to the others happens immediately, completely, and continuously.

Yet because we were created as distinct from God and endowed with free will, we cannot respond to the love of God as completely and simultaneously as the Persons of the Trinity. We need *time*— time to perceive God's love, time to understand it, time to accept it (or not). Finally, we need time to respond, to turn toward or away from Him:

> Our human reply cannot all at once be this total gift of
> ourselves, as prompt and immediate as God's offer of his
> love to us [. . .] God communicates himself to us gradually
> so that we can learn to grow at our own pace in response to
> him. This gradual and slow movement in response to God is
> equivalent to time.[40]

When I showed this quotation to a friend, Staniloae's words helped her make sense of something that has always troubled her: the plain and simple reality that human love always has a sense of limitation and finitude compared to the immeasurable nature of God's love. She explained that she hadn't realized this limitation was a matter of time. The Trinity being outside of time means that this Love is always present, always extant. "Being creatures in time," she wrote to me, "means that Love is layered like a cake: there is a beginning, a middle, and an end—not in the sense of a relationship ending, but as in an aim or telos. The end of any relationship is its fullness, or the extent of fullness we can experience as a finite being."[41] Her words made an impression on me: we need time to get as close as we can to the fullness of love, at least if we still want to retain the gift of personhood and free will while doing so. Since we are not God, it seems most fitting for such an endeavor to play out gradually, progressively, temporally.

Put another way, time—for God—is "the interval of waiting between knocking at our door and the moment when we will open it wide to him."[42] And God isn't the only one who knocks at our door—sometimes it's our neighbor, our spouse, or a total stranger. Sometimes we are the ones knocking on the door, waiting for someone to open. In those encounters, too, the loop of love—giving and responding—unfolds in time and is an equally meaningful component of our lives in Christ.

To paint Staniloae's relational view of time in earthly colors, I cannot help but see a similar process at work as I write this book. Among other things, writing a book is an act of love—a giving of oneself to one's audience. And while I hesitate to compare my

mental processes to the perfect communion of the Holy Trinity, there is nonetheless a kind of intrapersonal responsiveness in my mind, instantaneous and
ongoing. As I consider what this chapter
should say, one corner of my mind puts
an idea out there, another corner hears
and responds and builds on that idea,
and that process unfolds as I go about
my work. It's not unlike a conversation:
a call out into the world, a response, fol-

∿

*"Time is the interval of
waiting between God
knocking at our door and
the moment when we will
open it wide to him."*
—*Dumitru Staniloae*

∿

lowed by a counter-response—all bound up in time. It is a broken and human reflection of love, but nonetheless it is real and
meaningful.

The ultimate hope is that this internal dialogue becomes exter-
nalized in the form of words and sentences. That is a long and
laborious process, and at least in that regard, a book (and most
other human manifestations of love) differs from God's love.
Our act of self-giving is a hard-earned fight through the dense
jungle of ego and cognitive disconnects; God's is natural and
immediate. Nevertheless, all this hard work of writing is necessary so that someday—long in the future—these words can find
their way into your hands. Maybe some other day even further
in the future, you will respond to this act of love by recalling it
kindly, remembering me in your prayers, writing me a letter, rat-
ing this book on Amazon.com, or liking my page on Facebook.
Even if you don't, there was love given and freedom to respond.
And somehow, time was necessary for both of us to be included
in those things while still retaining our own unique identities.

THREE MODES OF TIME

When we begin to understand time as the vehicle for relationship and communion, time becomes evident in three modes: potential time, unfulfilled time, and actualized time. I have already alluded to potential time, namely the reality that all moments in time (chronos) carry the potential to be vessels of the eternal (kairos). Time as potential places us at a crossroad in every new moment that unfolds. Potential time becomes actualized (kairos) when we respond to God's love. In these moments of response, we partake of eternity, which consists of unity between persons in the bond of mutually self-giving love.[43] They pull us into the life-giving movement of God and eternal, self-sacrificial love. Actualized time is the true "real-time," because it is the only sense in which time becomes real or creative and life-giving, "a movement of the person beyond himself, in order to reduce the distance between himself and God" or his neighbor.[44]

By contrast, potential time becomes unfulfilled when we choose to spend it in unloving, un-self-giving ways:

> Time which is only an interval between a person and the things he wants to snatch or between himself and other persons considered as things to be dominated and exploited, is not properly time at all; it is simply a going forward in the desert of oneself towards total death.[45]

This state of being is unlike time because it terminates in total death, a condition in which there is no change or progress—we have "finally and definitively shut ourselves up in our own solitude where there is no call and no possibility of response any more [sic]."[46] This is a life lived *incurvatus in se*, a phrase St.

Augustine coined to denote a state of being turned inward toward the self rather than outward toward others and God. Like a shaving of wood, we become curled around our inner emptiness, to borrow an image that has been attributed to both St. Augustine and St. Theophan.

The destructive stagnancy of unfulfilled time is reminiscent of the Slough of Despond in John Bunyan's famous allegory *The Pilgrim's Progress*. En route to the Celestial City, Christian falls into a bog, where the weight of his sins and temptations pulls him deeper into the mire so he cannot move. It is a dark place, reminiscent of the slimy abyss and miserable pit spoken of in the Psalms (Ps. 39/40:2). Christian is eventually rescued by Help, who informs him that "[t]his miry slough is such a place as cannot be mended: it is the descent whither the scum and filth that attends conviction for sin doth continually run; and therefore it is called the Slough of Despond."[47]

To turn inward toward ourselves and our sins is to fall into our own proverbial slough of despond. In this mode of being, it is not so much that we waste time as that we turn time into a prison, enslaving us to the worst and most insular tendencies in ourselves. Eventually, we (like the fabled Narcissus) become virtually incapable of true relationship—with God or with anyone else.

TO RESPOND OR DESPOND?

As pointed out earlier, *acedia*—the Greek term for despondency favored by the theologians of late antiquity—connotes the absence of care. In regard to time, however, despondency also manifests itself as a lack of responsiveness. Actualized time consists of *re*-sponding, unfulfilled time of *de*-sponding. Both words—*respond* and *despond*—contain the Latin verb *spondere*: "to pledge, promise, or guarantee." To *re*-spond literally means to make a fresh promise. When we respond to God's love, we are essentially re-promising, re-giving ourselves—offering back to God what was given to us. It implies we are continuing or renewing something we have already done in the past. As has already been discussed, we do not have the capacity to give ourselves fully and completely. We respond to God again and again, re-giving and re-pledging ourselves in each new moment that unwinds from the scroll of time.

On the other hand, to *de*-spond means to lower or cancel a promise. It implies an absence of, or movement downward from, promise. And when we move away from response, when we descend from the opportunity to offer ourselves back to God—who is substance and fullness—our only option is emptiness. Death.

For a long time, I assumed that the palpable manifestations of despondency—anxiety, distraction, despair, among others— come first and themselves cause the soul to drift away from God and man. *If I could just be less anxious or distractible,* I have often thought, *I would be less despondent.* Cajoling oneself into proper behavior is usually not successful in the long term, and gradually I realized that the anxiety and distraction are merely coping mechanisms to mask a deeper and more painful reality about myself: a subtle but nonetheless persistent refusal to love, to care, to burden myself with reality. A refusal to "realize life," once again reiterating the words of Emily in *Our Town.* I don't think I'm unique in this; to a certain extent this is the epitome of our broken condition. But to begin to see this ugliness within oneself is at once clarifying and harrowing.

Perhaps despondency devolves into a more chronic condition after we have de-sponded to the love of God (or man) one too many times, thereby creating a habitual emptiness within ourselves that cuts us off from community. The outward accoutrements of despondency—the worry, the slackness, the distraction—seem to me like the mind's way of shoring up the shame that creeps in once we've stepped outside the garden of relationship, connection, and love. This

Despondency is not the most fashionable sin—it is stagnant self-absorption, desperate and isolating. If our bouts with it were occasional, we could sweep them under the carpet of "anger" or "pride"—not lesser sins, but perhaps a bit more on the glamorous side.

picture of things is a game-changer: no longer are anxious worries and distractions something to bludgeon out of ourselves. Rather, like the surge of pain we feel when touching a hot stove, they draw our attention to a deeper anti-movement within us: the habit of approaching time's potential in an apathetic, self-focused way.

This first occurred to me when I was standing in an elevator. I hate elevators. More specifically, I hate having to wait for people to get on and off the elevator, an experience I face multiple times a day living in a high-rise apartment building. This daily ordeal brings out the worst in me—I have glowered, I have rolled my eyes, I have sighed in contempt at strangers whose only misstep was needing to use the elevator at the same time as Her Royal Highness (me). My excuse was that they were wasting my time, and wasted time makes me anxious. But willing myself to stop stressing about the almighty Schedule only left me feeling more frantic than before.

Then, one day, I failed to hold the elevator door open for someone running to catch it. With a triumphant buoyancy, I watched the man hurry toward doors sliding shut—I didn't so much as lift a finger to stop them. As I and the otherwise empty elevator ascended to my apartment, a dark anxiety descended upon me—the same angst that always crept into my crabby elevator moments. *Why am I stressed out?* I wondered. *I'm not even waiting for anyone now.* That's when the light went on for me: my elevator angst was less a stress response to wasting time and more the aftershocks of my nastiness toward others. I began to observe my feelings and reactions in the coming days. It always happened so fast, but it was true: I felt more anxious after a moment of cruelty, even if my cruelty resulted in saving time. It forced me to conclude that my recurrent elevator anxiety had little to do with a squandered schedule and much more to do with the effort it took to act like a civil human being in the elevator rather than a crazed time snatcher.

Of course, none of this is easy to share, but I'm not alone in these tendencies. Not everyone has to wait for an elevator every day, but there are grocery lines and strong-willed toddlers and traffic jams. All of human development can be summed up as the process of learning we are not the sole protagonist in the story—other people exist. Despondency is not the most fashionable sin—it is stagnant self-absorption, desperate and isolating. If our bouts with it were occasional, we could sweep them under the carpet of "anger" or "pride"—not lesser sins, but perhaps a bit more on the glamorous side. In fact, in some ways these sins are easier to wrestle with because they are energetic passions—they involve a surge of something welling up within us, pushing us to do something. At times we can harness the energy of anger, for instance, and steer it in a more charitable direction in the form of advocacy or good works. But despondency is not just less energetic, it is energy-sucking. To wrestle against it requires first summoning within us the baseline spiritual vitality it perpetually robs us of. This, I think, is why despondency is rarely a "one-time offense," as anger tends to be, or even a series of repeat offenses, but rather a static, stubborn condition of the heart we can scarcely parse into distinct actions or choices.

This cesspool of stagnant carelessness cuts us off from the fullness of relationship. It punches holes in our experiences so that whatever is left of eternity quickly drains out of our time. Not that we must be bubbly, effusive extroverts full of warm fuzzies. Loving your neighbor, my spiritual father reminds me, isn't a feeling but an action—and usually not a showy one. The moments we spend grumbling about God or our fellow man are moments we failed to act—we failed to love or respond to love. I'm convinced that however justified we may feel in forsaking those moments, our hearts are traumatized by the way they cut us off from God, our neighbor, and our true selves. Despondency takes full force when that sense of trauma is consistently ignored in favor of apathy, anger, or desire.

TIME AND TRANSFORMATION

The title of an essay by Kallistos Ware crystalizes the existential predicament of time: "Time: Prison or Path to Freedom?"[48] Is time a downward spiral leading to death, or an upward ascent leading to life? Is it a mode of enslavement or one that leads to greater liberty, actualization, and relationship? In a sense, it is both—or rather, it has the potential to be either.

Along with being the dimensional fabric necessary for relationship, time opens a possibility that otherwise would be
unavailable to us: the chance to change. At first glance, change
is an unlikely thing for a mere mortal to praise—the ancients,
we have said, disparaged change as the dark force behind decay,
death, and motion. It is easy to forget that change leads not
only to death but also to life. After all, a seed must *change over
time* if it is ever to mature and yield fruit. What would life be
without change? In short, nothing—a world void of alteration
would be a barren one. "Eternity is life and life is movement,"
wrote Staniloae. Even God is characterized by a certain degree
of change inasmuch as He is love, which is quintessentially
dynamic rather than static: "The Holy Trinity remains eternally
unchangeable in its love, but its love is fullness of life and therefore there is inexhaustible potential for variation in its manifes-
tation and action."[49]

For anyone in the midst of despondency, this translates to an
important realization: where there is time and change, there is
the possibility for transformation—a way out of our despondent
prison is available. We must recover this reality for ourselves, as
despondency "constantly convinces us that no change is possible
and therefore desirable."[50] Until the last tick of the last clock, until
the last breath on our last day, there is reason to hope. Creation
was fashioned in such a way that we are never stranded within
our worst selves forever, at least not against our will—as long as
we are in time, we always have some step forward we can take,
however insignificant or impossible that step may seem. In this
regard, transformation depends just as much on us as it does on

God. The space we have in which to act is the freedom time opens to us, and one that is particularly necessary to remember in the midst of despondency.

How will we respond to the new moments, the new possibilities that are placed before us? Will we respond or despond? In *Man's Search for Meaning*, Viktor Frankl wrote, "Everything can be taken from a man but one thing: the last of the human freedoms—to choose one's attitude in any given set of circumstances."[51] Lest these words be dismissed as cliché, it's worth mentioning that Frankl honed his thinking on human psychology while a prisoner in Auschwitz. Whenever I make excuses for my attitude, this quotation offers a suitable reality check.

Since we are on the subject of Frankl, allow me to share another excerpt, this time on the topic of love. In his book, Frankl recalls a grueling march he and some fellow prisoners were forced to endure. While they were being pushed through the icy darkness amid stones and large puddles, the man marching next to Frankl wondered aloud how their wives were doing in their camp and hoped they had no idea what the men had to suffer. From that moment, Frankl and this man were silently preoccupied, thinking of their wives and the love they shared. This simple act of remembrance fortified the men for the rest of the march. Frankl comments:

> A thought transfixed me: for the first time in my life I saw
> the truth as it is set into song by so many poets, proclaimed
> as the final wisdom by so many thinkers. The truth—that
> love is the ultimate and the highest goal to which man can
> aspire. Then I grasped the meaning of the greatest secret
> that human poetry and human thought and belief have to

impart: *The salvation of man is through love and in love.* I
understood how a man who has nothing left in this world
still may know bliss, be it only for a brief moment, in the
contemplation of his beloved. In a position of utter desola-
tion, when man cannot express himself in positive action,
when his only achievement may consist in enduring his
sufferings in the right way—an honorable way—in such
a position man can, through loving contemplation of the
image he carries of his beloved, achieve fulfillment. For the
first time in my life I was able to understand the meaning of
the words, "The angels are lost in perpetual contemplation
of an infinite glory."[52]

What can one say in response to such pivotal words? I am struck
by the beauty of Frankl's experience, particularly love's ability
to transfigure an otherwise harrowing ordeal. Given the choice,
Frankl opted to dwell in the love of his wife rather than in bitterness or hatred toward his oppressors. In that moment, he realized something of what it's like for the angels to contemplate the
divinity of God. Frankl goes so far as to say that our salvation
lies in love, a point that holds particular hope for despondency.
If the simple, human act of love is enough to spare someone from
the poisonous bitterness of oppression, it is more than capable of
raising us from our slimy sloughs.

But love, like so many other things, is a learning process, one
that takes our whole lives and beyond. When I talk to people
about the personal ramifications of despondency, I often detect
a sense of failure in their voices. Many of us know at least some
of what we could do to avoid despondency, but we find ourselves
giving in to the same old temptations over and over again. In
some ways, it would be easier to live in a world in which eternity

was at a distance, located in some future iteration of reality. In that world, there would be little harm in procrastinating in our battle for wholeness. In that world, we could afford to bide our time however we chose. In our world, however, every moment—every *now*—is an invitation to abide in the love of Christ. To put off the moment-by-moment effort of responding to this love amounts to no less than rejecting the "today" of salvation (2 Cor. 6:2), and with it, salvation itself.[53]

This is a sobering prospect, particularly in the context of despondency, where procrastination is something of a default. At the risk of minimizing its significance in the spiritual life, however, it is worth remembering that the same potentiality of time we so easily reject is also a vessel of grace. I am reminded of the parable of the workers in the vineyard, in which Christ compares the Kingdom of heaven to a master who pays a full day's wages even to laborers who were hired in the final hour of work (see Matt. 20:1–16). Whether you are in the first or the eleventh hour of your despondency, if you wish to labor in the vineyard, all you need to do is enter.

I like to think of time as the giver of second chances—and seventy-seventh chances, too. Second chances are powerful and life-giving because they allow us to recover time that has been lost, or at least time we thought was lost. They lend us new eyes to envision a more spacious future, a possibility that may not have been available to us before we were given a second chance. In relationships, second chances occur only once in a while, but in time, they are granted perpetually. Every moment that trickles forth from the reservoir of time is a new, fresh possibility that wasn't there before. Yet it may not always appear that way. Instead of the reservoir of second chances, time may seem rather like the giver of more of the same—more of the same old drudgery, the same old mistakes, the same old hurts. We must cling to the knowledge, though, that time doesn't keep score or award us based on merit; it dishes out yet another moment just as ripe with possibility as the last, regardless of how many similar moments we've squandered before.

When God's love seems like an unlikely hypothetical, it helps to consider time and the way it carries us forward, regardless of how badly we've screwed things up (again). Time asks no questions and makes no judgments; it takes my hand, beckons me one step forward, and says, "Here is something new for you: this moment." Admittedly, there are instances when this forward-moving thrust of time is painful—when we've lost a loved one, for example, and each tick of the clock rips us further from the last day that person was alive in the flesh. Still, there are many other times when it is good and healing to realize we do not have to stay stuck in one place. Moments of despondency comprise some of the instances when I find myself most grateful for time's stubborn, forward-moving grace.

CONCLUSION

In many ways, despondency results from our own blindness to the beauty of love enfolded in "every, every minute" of our lives. It arises from our neglect of time's potential. Emily's failure in *Our Town* to fully "realize" the potential of so many moments in her life resembles the condition of humanity—even the best of us are prone to taking for granted the many opportunities we have to love and respond to love. From a spiritual perspective, we understand that this ordinary human tendency can grow into something much more pernicious and destructive. The sickness of despondency is a turning inward, confining ourselves to the insular and ungrateful life of the self and to the emptiest aspects of time on earth. Resembling the dead in the *Our Town* cemetery, we become bound to our prison and oriented toward the abyss of solitary darkness.

The opposite of this despondent condition is not happiness nor jubilation, but rather love—a turning outward from the self to one's neighbor, God, and eternity. The latter is crucial; in the view of the Church Fathers, the "every, every minute" we fail to realize in this life consists not merely of love or beauty but of eternity itself. Time, then, becomes not only the vehicle of relationship and eternity, but the path of transformation we can travel to get there. From this vantage point, time—for all its repetition—becomes not a fatal loop of mortality but an upward spiral, a "never-ending dance of love, drawing us 'farther up and farther in[to]'" the eternally loving God.[54] However often we may fall backward in this life, time remains the path waiting and willing to press us forward.

CHAPTER 3

What Is the Present Moment?

True happiness is to enjoy the present, without anxious
dependence upon the future, not to amuse ourselves with
either hopes or fears but to rest satisfied with what we have.

—SENECA, *OF A HAPPY LIFE* I

DESPONDENCY IS THE MOST TEMPORAL OF THE PASSIONS. It severs our relationship to time; rather than a mode of transformation and ongoing resurrection, time becomes our enemy, a prison that holds us captive to our own self-destruction. When time drags on slowly, our life's activities—especially prayer—stagnate. When time hastens, it confronts us with the brevity and transience of the things we love. Soon, we are exhausted by the mere idea of seeing tasks to completion.

At the epicenter of our splintered relationship to time lies a rejection of the present moment. Ultimately, despondency signals an escape from the gift of God's ongoing self-revelation, the gift of love He bestows upon us at each juncture of our lives, not the least of which is His presence in time through Christ.

Presentist mantras resound from all corners of today's culture—"Stay in the present!" "Live in the moment!" These slogans often function as shorthand admonishments to stop stressing out or getting caught up in worry. On one level, this conventional call to stay in the present is not such a bad thing—it's generally healthier to focus on what is actually in front of us rather than to fixate on what is not. Yet these cursory sayings also mask a certain emptiness. In our postmodern conceptions, the ideal substance of the "present moment" is a vacant space—empty of our worries and anxieties, yes, and in some extremes even empty of our very selves. (In transcendental meditation and certain Eastern religions, for example, the extinction of self is seen as the pinnacle of enlightenment.)

As a teenager, I once attended a fitness class at an ordinary community-center gym. That morning, we were told, the class was to conclude with a relaxation session. We lay on our mats with our eyes closed while the instructor guided us through a meditation and told us to visualize ourselves alone in an empty room, free of whatever worries we had brought to class. We practiced mentally letting go of anxieties one by one until, eventually, we were coaxed to visualize the room as a complete void—empty of even ourselves, as though our very presence were corrupting this pure, empty space. It was strangely jarring and discombobulating—I had to leave the class early.

I never quite knew what to make of this experience until, years later, I came across these words by St. Theophan the Recluse:

> Solitude is not a mere vacuum nor can it be gained simply by creating complete emptiness in oneself. When you retreat into yourself, you should stand before the Lord, and remain in His presence. [. . .] This is the true wilderness— to stand face to face with the Lord. The state of standing before the Lord is something that supports and maintains itself.[55]

To paraphrase St. Theophan's message, in the light of Christ, reality consists not of emptiness but of fullness. Christ, the Divine Liturgy of St. Basil asserts, descended "into Hades through the Cross, that He might fill all things with Himself," even hell itself. The Resurrection of Christ was also the resurrection and filling of all things. Time is no longer the harbinger of death—it has been conquered, or rather resurrected, to its prototype: eternity. To "live in the present," for the Christian, is to dwell in this fullness. From such a vantage point, the present is less a duration of time and more a state of being—one that is not measured by clocks or ascertained by the mind but experienced by the heart.

Another way of describing this state of being present in the heart is what the *Philokalia*—one of the most beloved devotional texts in Eastern Christianity—calls *nepsis* (νῆψις), a prayerful inner watchfulness.[56] The English translation of the *Philokalia* defines *nepsis* as "the opposite to a state of drunken stupor; hence spiritual sobriety, alertness, vigilance." Being present in this way "signifies an attitude of attentiveness [. . .] whereby one keeps watch over one's inward thoughts and fantasies, [. . .] maintaining guard over the heart and intellect."[57] Nepsis fuels a mindful, peaceful, yet alert stance toward one's immediate experiences. Its aim, however, is not therapeutic but spiritual—watchfulness creates space within the heart to receive truth, to pray unceasingly, and to confess Christ:

> Watchfulness is a way of embracing every virtue, every
> commandment. It is the heart's stillness and, when free from
> mental images, it is the guarding of the intellect. [. . .] [It is]
> unbroken by any thought. In this stillness the heart breathes
> and invokes, endlessly and without ceasing, only Jesus

Christ who is the Son of God and Himself God. It confesses
Him who alone has power to forgive our sins, and with His
aid it courageously faces its enemies. Through this invoca-
tion enfolded continually in Christ, who secretly divines all
hearts, the soul does everything it can to keep its sweetness
and its inner struggle hidden from men, so that the devil,
coming upon it surreptitiously, does not lead it into evil and
destroy its precious work.[58]

The essence of nepsis, then, is prayer. To be present is to pray,
"to stand with the mind in the heart before God, and to go on
standing before Him unceasingly day and night, until the end of
life."[59]

Why is it so crucial to "be present" in the way St. Theophan
and the neptic Fathers admonish? Because the present moment
is the only time in which we can encounter the Resurrection and
Christ Himself. We cannot meet Him in the past or future; the
only time we have is now. As proclaimed in Psalm 118(119):126 (a
verse that traditionally commenced the Divine Liturgy), "[Now]
It is time for the Lord to act."[60] The Greek word for *time* in this
context is *kairos* (see Chapter 2); invoking these words prior to
eucharistic services converges the liturgical present with eternity.
By extension, now is also the time for *us* to act, in synergy and
cooperation with God, and it is the only time we have been given
in which to do so.

Nonetheless, the mind or intellect—the rational, thinking
energy of the human person—avoids the present moment. Archimandrite Meletios Webber explains that we prefer to dwell on the
past or future (or at least our ideations thereof) because the present moment

has no shape or form, so there is nothing to measure. Since
defining things through labeling and measuring is the main
task of the mind, when it comes to something formless, it
simply ignores it. The mind prefers to work in the past or
future, since these dimensions are both actually constructs
of the mind's own workings and thus the mind can control
them. The present moment, however, is completely outside
its control and therefore completely ignored.[61]

Because the direct experience of reality is difficult to control
or categorize, the mind entices us into worries, fears, regrets,
desires, ambitions, or fantasies—modes of engaging not the
present, but our fabricated sense of past or future. Thus are our
years "spent in thought like a spider" (Ps. 89/90:9), trapped in the
filaments of our own mind. We cringe at an embarrassing mem
ory from childhood; we fantasize about a promotion we hope to
attain; we become angry all over again at something our spouse
said years ago.

Although such ruminations may cause us pain, it is a pain the
mind itself creates and is therefore preferable to the unpredictable
vulnerability of the present moment. To root ourselves in the here
and now means to surrender to uncertainty and, at times, help-
lessness. We are forced to acknowledge we actually care about
something, and caring is a painful business. Kathleen Norris
writes:

That it hurts to care is borne out in etymology, for *care*
derives from an Indo-European word meaning "to cry out,"
as in lament. Caring is not passive, but an assertion that no
matter how strained and messy our relationships can be, it
is worth something to be present, with others, doing our

small part. Care is also required for the daily routines that [despondency] would have us suppress or deny as meaning-less repetition or too much bother.[62]

Perhaps the first step of despondency—the first departure from the present moment—is numbing ourselves to care and all the pain it can bring. Counterintuitive though it may seem, foster-ing regret and anxiety toward past and future are part of that numbing process, because they extract us from the arena of car-ing and deposit us in the cesspool of rumination, where the mind can manipulate its own reality. Ultimately, we find ourselves dis-dainful of the present, consumed by thoughts that combine "an undercurrent of negativity or dissatisfaction with a sense that the reality of God's world is not good enough."[63] We desire to be "anywhere but here; any moment but now."[64]

If we are to overcome this dissatisfaction, we must find our way back to whatever it means to be present. The Person of Christ—the Love of God revealed—is our guide. Although "Christ *is* the same yesterday, today, and forever" (Heb. 13:8), His presence in time is a sacred mystery that unfolds in infinite particularities through the course of each life. Christ is, in short, the manifes-tation of God's love as action. The present moment is the space in which His (and our) action can take place—the kind of action that demands that love mature from a state of passive being into something relational and visible (see Chapter 2).

Nonetheless, the exact image of that kind of love is different for each of us and is constantly developing as each present moment evolves into the next. Sometimes, the present may consist of a person—a child who needs caring for, an isolated individual seeking community, or a coworker who insists on having a conversation before we've had a chance to imbibe our third cup of coffee. Sometimes, we may be that person in need, learning lessons of humility and love as we depend on the graciousness of others. On still other occasions, the present moment consists of a task we have been avoiding, a passion that needs dealing with, a meal that needs cooking, a pile of clothes that needs laundering.

Most often, though, the present appears to consist of nothing—nothing particularly immediate to accomplish, nothing that entices our attention, nothing that seems meaningful or significant. In my experience, these moments of apparent nothingness leave us more susceptible to despondency than busier and more purposeful times. The ability to face the Bermuda-triangle moments of our existence—to acknowledge the pain of disorienting pointlessness and endeavor to find fullness in the vacant margins of life—is as important as how we respond to an abundance of monumental tasks.

A psychologist friend once told me an anecdote that illustrates the need to make peace with time's empty spaces. Many years ago, when he began his residency training, he moved his family—his wife and their young children—to the suburbs of a large city. Once a week, his wife would pack up the kids and travel by bus into the city to have lunch with him at work. This was always a challenging ordeal for her, not only for all the obvious reasons life with young ones entails, but also because the buses were driven at breakneck speed—passengers had to take precautions not to be thrown around whenever the bus came to a stop. At first, the wife accepted this as a reality of urban driving—until she realized that the buses traveled even more erratically than any of the surrounding traffic. She finally commented on this to one of the drivers.

∾

If we cannot learn to dwell in the seeming emptiness of the present, we will never encounter its fullness.

∾

"We're kind of stuck between a rock and a hard spot," the driver responded, as though he'd heard the complaint before. He explained that when the city planners had created the bus schedules, they only recorded how much time it took to get from one stop to another—forgetting to factor in the time needed for the bus to actually stop and pick passengers up or drop them off. Until new plans were developed, the bus drivers in this city sped around so they would not fall behind schedule.

My friend tells this story when he wants to help people remember how much of life is lived in the margins of time—the events we don't put on our calendars, the chance meetings we didn't plan for, the things we encounter rather than accomplish. The present moment is like those unaccounted-for bus stops—junctures we were meant to stop at and fulfill the purpose of our trip. Like the city planners in my friend's old city, we become so focused on getting to the next big thing that we overlook the time we are given to actually be where we're supposed to be on this earthly journey. If we cannot learn to dwell in the seeming emptiness of the present, we will never encounter its fullness.

CHAPTER 4

Escaping the Present

Remember then: there is only one time that is important—
Now! It is the most important time because it is the only
time when we have any power.

—LEO TOLSTOY, "THE THREE QUESTIONS"[65]

Trust no Future, howe'er pleasant!
Let the dead Past bury its dead!
Act—act in the living Present!
Hearth within, and God o'erhead!

—HENRY WADSWORTH LONGFELLOW, "A PSALM OF LIFE"[66]

ST. JOHN CASSIAN, A CONTEMPORARY OF EVAGRIUS, devoted an entire book of his lengthy *Institutes* to the sin of despondency (acedia). At the beginning of this book, he listed various symptoms of this destructive state of being. What is striking in this enumeration is the frequency with which Cassian alluded to the tendency for struggling monks to flee their surroundings—the monastic cell, their companions, or the monastery in general.

"When [despondency] has taken possession of some unhappy soul," he wrote, "it produces dislike of the place, disgust with the cell, and disdain and contempt of the brethren who dwell with him or at a little distance." Likewise, despondency "does not

75

suffer [the monk] to stay in his cell," but instead causes him to believe "he will never be well while he stays in that place, unless he leaves his cell." To justify the desire to go elsewhere, "the disease suggests that he ought to show courteous and friendly hospitalities to the brethren, and pay visits to the sick, whether near at hand or far off." And even when the monk remains in his cell, despondency produces in him a kind of restlessness reminiscent of a caged tiger: "[The monk] looks about anxiously this way and that, and sighs that none of the brethren come to see him, and often goes in and out of his cell, and frequently gazes up at the sun, as if it was too slow in setting, and so a kind of unreasonable confusion of mind takes possession of him like some foul darkness."[67]

The monk's proclivity for being on the move—for leaving his dwelling place—surfaces and resurfaces in Cassian's writing with a redundancy that frustrates my editorial sensibilities. But it probably conveys an important realization about despondent habits—and not just for idle monks of a bygone era. When I think back on the places and spaces I have ever been tempted to flee—traffic jams come to mind—they all boil down to temporality, not geography. In other words, it isn't the space itself I want to run away from but the time that traps me in that space: the present moment. The uncertainty of the present moment confronts us with an ever-unfolding reminder that we are not God, that we are not the masters of our own universe, that there are things we cannot choose or control.

Whatever the present looks like at any given moment, there are only two possible ways of responding to it: to enter or exit it, to respond or despond. To enter the present is to surrender with thanksgiving to the time and circumstances God has placed before us, to abide in God's presence in time and space. To exit, by contrast, is to reject this gift—really, to reject reality. Despondency begins when we step away from the present and fashion reality on our own terms.

As I see it, there are three primary avenues of escape: physical, mental, and spiritual. Although these groupings are not strict categories, they provide a basis for parsing and recognizing the common loopholes by which we—like the despondent monk Cassian described—wiggle our way out of the here and now.

MAKING THE ESCAPE: PHYSICALLY

> *Whenever it begins in any degree to overcome any one, it [. . .] drives him out from [his cell] and makes him restless and a wanderer, and indolent in the matter of all kinds of work, and it makes him continually go round [to] the cells of the brethren and the monasteries.*
>
> —ST. JOHN CASSIAN[68]

Physical escapes from the present are visible and obvious. In ascetical theology, there is a metaphor that to me exemplifies this mode of escape, namely that of a monk who leaves his private cell to visit his brothers. One also reads of despondent monks fleeing from the monastic setting altogether to visit their "relatives in the world."[69] This verbal image reminds us that the first and most recognizable escape from the present is made physically, by manipulating our immediate spatial environment.

The despondent monk's impetuous comings and goings were antithetical to the ethos of monasticism in late antiquity, which adhered to the so-called stability of place (*stabilitas loci*).[70]

According to this concept, once a monk entered a particular monastery, he was expected to remain there for the rest of his earthly life unless some extreme circumstance intervened. Stability of place was one facet of the obedience, humility, and spiritual martyrdom these early monastics strove to practice, and this may be why ascetical theologians like Cassian and Evagrius were so sensitive to the restive visitations of their brother monks. Even if a despondent brother obeyed the letter of monastic life by remaining within the community, his constant wanderings contradicted the spirit of stability.

In reading descriptions of this strange restlessness, I get the impression that it wasn't traveling or socializing that was most disconcerting, but rather the impulsivity and carelessness that accompanied it in the case of despondency. Fraternizing in the bond of Christian fellowship is one thing, but thoughtlessly using others as instruments to distract or entertain oneself is another. In the latter, the despondent monk shows little control over his actions—far from being intentional or loving in his relationships, he simply doesn't know what else to do with himself. His temptations lead him to distract not only himself but those around him.

We may not be monks living in desert caves, but countless delights entice us from our proverbial cells, that is, the places or tasks we are responsible for at any given moment. We call, we text, we busy ourselves with smartphones and email inboxes and mundane distractions. It's a beautiful thing to live in community with others, but how often do we participate in the social realm with love or mindfulness? What would it even mean to interact that way in a digital age?

As a freelance editor and consultant, I spend many of my working hours in front of a computer screen. As soon as I face some minute difficulty in a current project, I am visited by an almost frantic urge to find something else to do. *How wonderful it would be,* the thought often occurs to me, *to leave the cave of Microsoft Word and check in with my fellow monks in the Facebook cell.* Usually it all happens so quickly that I don't realize I've left my work cell until I'm on my third—or tenth—cute animal video.

Even aside from the internet, we still have more options for distraction than ever before, alternative cells to wander off to when life and its realities are too much. Consider the cell of gluttony ("emotional eating" in the language of self-help literature), or the cell of sleeping when not actually tired, the cell of television and Netflix, the cell of getting completely lost in a rumination. Finally, there's the cell of laziness and, by contrast, that of unnecessary busyness.

As with the socializing monks Evagrius wrote about, it is usually not the activities themselves that are "bad," but the thoughtless and ultimately self-serving ways we indulge in them. Even seemingly "good" or "healthy" activities can become avenues of escape when taken to an extreme—exercise, healthy eating, or cleaning. (Incidentally, my husband can usually tell when I've got a tough work assignment because he comes home to a multi-course dinner made from scratch and a suddenly pristine apartment.)

Of course, none of the cells listed above is strictly a physical or geographical space. The cells we wander off to have mental and spiritual (and, increasingly, digital) components, just as we are syntheses of mind, body, and soul. Nonetheless, in retreating to these activities, we reenact the despondent monk's anti-pilgrimage away from the cell he is called to be in and into alternative cells of distraction.

MAKING THE ESCAPE: MENTALLY

> *Looking at the sun, [the monk] concludes that the sun hardly moves or does not move at all, and he has the impression that the day is fifty hours long.*
>
> —EVAGRIUS[71]

Although physical escapes from the present are more obvious to an observer, they begin internally on the level of thought, particularly the intrusive logismoi mentioned in Chapter 1. Both Evagrius and St. John Cassian painted a picture of this tendency in describing a monk staring at the sun. This time, although the monk manages to remain in his cell, physically, his eyes (like his mind) are elsewhere.

Echoing Evagrius's portrayal, St. John wrote that the despondent monk "looks about anxiously this way and that [. . .] and frequently gazes up at the sun, as if it was too slow in setting."[72] This is someone who is anxious for time to pass, gazing at the sun as though trying to discover a loophole in the seemingly endless monotony of life. "From morning to evening, the day grinds on," writes Dennis Okholm, paraphrasing early ascetic depictions of despondency. "The monk keeps poking his head out of his cell to check the sun's position."[73]

Perhaps a more familiar image today would be a person who cannot stop checking the clock. The sun, after all, functioned as a timepiece—in Evagrius's day, the invention of mechanical clocks was still nearly a millennium away, and sundials would have been rare so far out in the desert. Yet it is not so much the passage of time the monk seeks, but the disruption and novelty time brings about as it unfolds. He scours the skies, waiting for the sun to budge so he can finally move on—to the next task, the next exercise, the next prayer, the next visit with someone. He is desperate for something—*anything*—to change, at the very least time itself.

Although he remains in his physical location, the monk described here escapes the present via anxiety, anticipation, and desire—habits of the mind we can all relate to. Whether it is twelve noon or twelve midnight, whether we live in a desert or a tundra, despondency makes it seem as though time is moving in an unacceptable manner. The sun-searching monk was perplexed by time's sluggishness, but moments when time seems to move too rapidly provoke a similar—albeit inverted—angst, revealing how little we have accomplished or completed. We grow restless and ruminative in the face of time's perceived slowness, sad and worried in its acceleration.

This poignant picture reminds us that *being* somewhere does not necessarily mean being *present* there. If we were to watch this monk from a distance, perhaps from our own solitary cell somewhere across the expanse of sun and sand, he would appear to be following the rules. We would not see a "tramper of steps," trotting to and fro from cave to endless cave of dissipation.[74] We might not detect his furtive glances at the sun nor hear the restive sighs of boredom. Yet this fellow is every bit as removed from the present as his brother monk who physically departs from the monastery. It is neither the sun nor time that is the monk's enemy, but his inward disposition, characterized by anxiety and desire.

Like him, we have many mental and emotional paths by which to slither out of the present moment: desire, regret, anxiety, and fear—ways of dwelling in our imaginations of past or future rather than the reality of the present. If you are unhappy and dissatisfied in your job, for instance, your thoughts might lead you to desire something better in the future. You start building up a fantasy-laden possibility in your mind, and before you know it, you have checked out of your present circumstances. On other occasions, your mind may adopt a more painful approach, feeding on regret for working at your current company, retracing all the mistakes and failures that led you here in the first place. In the former case, we are drawn into the future, in the latter back to the past.

A rude awakening often follows these momentary escapes— the phone rings, and we are jolted back into the present, only to find it has changed little in our absence. The more we build up our fantasies (even negative ones), the more intolerable the present becomes, because we cannot truly escape it—it devolves into a prison, locking us into a seeming lack of control or freedom. This is why even harsh, negative fantasies of the mind frequently appeal to us more than our actual circumstances: in our mind, we become the inventor and creator (and controller) of our despair.

On a deeper level, then, we can see in the monk's glances at the sun something of a path, an existential circuit, a shape that life conforms to when under the influence of despondency. Our thoughts take us down one mental rabbit hole after another, propelled by the illusion that all our imaginings will somehow change our present circumstances. One glance back at reality, however, indicates that life has not altered despite all our internal wanderings. Despair soon follows, and the mind tries to resolve or explain the situation with another fantasy. The more we travel along this circuit, the more our thoughts blindfold the heart, the eye of the soul.[75]

For Evagrius, knowing was equated with seeing, the act of perceiving through our soul.[76] When our spiritual vision has clouded, we become blind to God and blind to the nuances and undeserved goodness of our actual circumstances—like the sun in the sky, we get stuck in one place. But we are not truly stuck, nor does the sun actually fail to change position in the sky—what has gotten stuck is our heart. Just as the monk's cave of solitude becomes a jail cell, our heart's inner prayer chamber calcifies into a barren tomb.

Evagrius believed that despondency has two primary roots in the mind: desire and anger.[77] To be honest, I could not immediately understand how desire factors in—despondency, in my experience, consists far more of an absence of desire, a deadness of the will. However, the Dutch Catholic theologian Henri Nouwen reminds us that "being is desiring," that we cannot be alive without desire. Whenever desire seems to flag, we must take a closer look. As he sees it, when desire is exercised well, it teaches us to love and search for God. This is the longing, he says, that should "guide all other desires." Otherwise desire turns stale or restless, "leading to despair and self-destruction. Spiritual disciplines are not ways to eradicate all our desires but ways to order them so that they can serve one another and serve God."[78] When we grow disconnected from that primary desire to love others and journey toward God, everything within us devolves into a slow, subtle chaos.

Maybe the apparent *lack* of desire I long equated with despondency is not a true absence but rather a canceling out of too many conflicting, insistent desires clamoring for attention. Admittedly, the way I picture this is likely shaped by my favorite film, *Awakenings,* based on Oliver Sacks' book of the same title. It recounts his experience working with patients suffering from encephalitis, also known as the sleeping sickness. These patients spent much of their lives in what appeared to be a catatonic state, frozen in a rigid stillness.

Without spoiling the ending, suffice it to say that the outcome of the story hinges on Sacks' realization that the stillness of encephalitis was an advanced stage of the same tremors and twitches one sees in Parkinson's patients. Once tremors become severe enough, they gradually cancel each other out and cave in on one another, freezing the body in an immobile state. In some ways, despondency resembles encephalitis—from the outside, it looks like a complete cessation of desire. Upon closer inspection, however, it consists of too many unruly desires duking it out against one another and becoming frozen in a kind of rigid, disabled tension.

Anger is the other prong of despondency's origins, for Evagrius. This kind of anger, I think, steps in to reanimate us after our warring desires have come to an eerie standstill. Anger appeals to our animal (irrational) as well as our human (rational) natures—at times the object of our rage makes little sense but feels completely real and legitimate nonetheless. The anger of despondency is the anger of thwarted wishes, of reality not aligning with our silent demands—the anger that covers the pain of a lifetime spent trying (and failing) to be one's own god.

The aim of this discussion is not to minimize emotions or emotional responses to the logismoi—feelings are part of our makeup as human beings. Rather, I wish to recognize that emotions and thoughts are the driving force behind despondent tendencies. When patterns of the mind hold us hostage without our being aware of them, they wreak havoc with our perceptions. In recognizing such patterns, we begin to attend to them in a way that allows our souls to grow softer rather than harder, more in touch with reality rather than less. This is a theme that will unfold on a more practical level throughout the rest of this book.

MAKING THE ESCAPE: SPIRITUALLY

> *In particular, the demon of despondency creates listlessness when one rises for prayer. Then he bothers us again when we pray or psalmodize* [sic], *in that he urges us to hurry.*
> —EVAGRIUS[79]

Finally, despondency is marked by a tendency to withdraw spiritually from the present. In theological discourses, despondency is often described as the temptation to abandon what the Fathers call *askesis*—spiritual effort or discipline. It's a temptation that shows up in two dominant forms. On the one hand, we may gradually cease spiritual endeavors altogether. On the other hand, we may continue—or even intensify—going through the motions, but they eventually become absent of any true presence on our part.

Of the two tendencies, the most common is the first—despondency pulls us toward spiritual slackness, instilling within us a false but insistent sense of weariness.[80] As Evagrius describes, no sooner does a despondent monk embark upon the work of prayer than he feels mysteriously fatigued, although he scarcely knows why. In this stupor, he puts prayer off, sometimes indefinitely. When he finally does rise for nighttime prayers, despondency persuades him to go through the motions, to simply move his tongue a bit in his mouth rather than to actually pray.[81] This monk, of course, could be any of us. Over time, our shortcuts in prayer contribute to an attitude of minimalism that goes on to infect every other realm of life. We cut tiny corners here and there until very little remains of the meaningful, daily acts of "abiding" that graft us to Christ (John 15:4).

I find the picture of a lone monk in his cell touching—there he is, standing in his prayer corner before bed, wagging his little tongue in half-prayers. He is so close to communion with Christ—yet so far. Of course, prayers go beyond speech. They are something we *are*—or are becoming—and cannot be reduced to the things we merely say or repeat. Sacred silence can often be more "prayerful" than extended prayer soliloquies.

Yet if it is "what comes out of the mouth" that defiles us (Matt. 15:11), we should be vigilant of the times we mumble and rush the words of prayer. The Epistle of St. James reminds us that the tongue, despite being a "little member," is the most powerful part of the body (James 3:5). It is like a litmus test of our soul—if evil words escape our mouth, we must assume something is not quite right in our soul (3:9–12). Like a ship's rudder, the tongue steers us into unity or disunity with Christ and our neighbor (3:4). When St. James alludes to the destruction an "untamed" tongue can cause, I have always assumed he was talking about boasting and cursing—using the tongue to say too much. What about when the tongue says too little, particularly in prayer?

The lukewarm prayer of the despondent monk represents the countless spiritual avenues of escaping the present moment. Most obviously, we can simply turn our backs on Christ and His

Church. We can refuse to pray, go to church, honor the Lord's day. We can minimalize or ignore altogether the fasting seasons given to us by the Church. On a more subtle level, though, we can continue through the motions of all these activities—prayer, sacraments, fasting, almsgiving, church attendance—yet still flee from them in our minds. The prayers offered only by our lips and tongues neglect to drill down and draw life from our heart, where Christ dwells. How easy it is to stand in our icon corners and *say* prayers—how difficult it is to *live* them. Instead we flee to the self-constructed realm of ideas, fantasies, concerns, regrets.

Because the nous is so closely intertwined with the experience of God, the present moment of the spirit often seems more spacious, expansive, and eternal than the "moments" of the mind, ordinarily perceived as fleeting or instantaneous. I believe we have all had moments like this, junctures that seemed to usher us into a place and time bigger and more vast than our senses could communicate. Sometimes these moments come to us without our doing much—the birth of a child, the death of a loved one, the timely meeting of a wise stranger. These are moments that hold something of eternity in them. Most often, however, living in the mystery of the present moment requires a bit of work on our part, askesis. Ordinarily, it is simply easier to stay in the ruminations of the mind than the stillness of the heart.

In this instance, the Church remains a willing aid, ready to lead us by the hand back to the present. In previous chapters, I mentioned one reason it is difficult to stay in the present: it is nebulous and evades measurement. However, the liturgical and doxological frameworks of the Church lend experiential structure and meaning to the present—the Church fills real time with the

∽

Every juncture of sacred time links us to the Incarnation, the reaching of eternity into this world, and in doing so, unites us not only to Christ but to the realization of our very selves as icons of Him.

∽

substance of salvation. Special prayers and services mark the different times of day, days of the week, and periods of the year. There are seasons of fasting and feasting, kneeling and standing. There are saints' days and feasts to commemorate the critical events of Christ's life. Every day, every moment is accounted for in the Church, and not just on an abstract level but physically and concretely through the fasts, feasts, and seasons, all of which seek to manifest Christ in and through time.

The Church calls not just our minds but our whole being and all our wandering loose ends back into existence, back into presence. In this way, the timekeeping of the Church reaches beyond that of the clock, which provides little more than an abstract framework to partition time into quantities. Every juncture of sacred time links us to the Incarnation, the reaching of eternity into this world, and in doing so, unites us not only to Christ but to the realization of our very selves as icons of Him.

This chapter has outlined some of the avenues by which we escape the present via the body, mind, and soul, fusing ourselves more closely to the demon of despondency. Yet virtually any activity in life can become a way to escape the present. Fortunately, though, it is equally true that every activity in life—from prayer to partaking of food to watching films—can reunite us with the present.

By way of anecdote, my spiritual father is one of the wisest people in my life—and he is also the biggest film buff I know. Sometimes, when I am back in town, I will watch a film with him and Presbytera. But we do not just watch them—we pay attention to them, we discuss them. Some of those films have taught me much about God and what it means to be human. To me, that sort of watchfulness over ourselves and the human condition is the beginning of the path that leads us out of despondency.

Most any ordinary activity, when approached with a clean heart, can become the first step back to reality and vigilance. The point is not to denigrate the particular movements or escape routes we have discussed thus far. The real enemy here is the impulsive, dissatisfied default of despondency—the desire to live anywhere but the present we are faced with (by which I mean, of course, the gift of reality we are given by God on a continual basis for our salvation).

The next few chapters explore how this default can be countered—the various antidotes the desert fathers and others have prescribed against despondency, all of which involve some aspect of reclaiming the present moment in our lives.

PART II

RECLAIMING THE PRESENT

Stepping Stones on the Path
Out of Despondency

CHAPTER 5

Prayer and Despondency

When true simplicity is gained,
To bow and to bend we shan't be ashamed,
To turn, turn will be our delight,
Till by turning, turning we come 'round right.

—SHAKER FOLK SONG

I pray once more, Awesome One,
Again You hear me through the wind....

Now I am assembled again
from all the pieces of my shame....
I count up the sum of myself, my God, and You,
You have the right to spend it.

—RAINER MARIA RILKE,
"ICH BETE WIEDER, DU ERLAUCHTER..."[82]

IN THE HAZE OF DESPONDENCY, PRAYER BECOMES BOTH the most difficult and the most vital endeavor. It hardly comes easily to the soul that is slackened. We listen as wiser souls—like sojourners reporting back from some beautiful, distant land— regale us with the riches of prayer. They speak of demons fought, of light encountered and happiness found. Hearing their travel tales makes us long to know prayer like that—prayer that is not just something we suspect we ought to do, but a journey toward a new way of being, a new mode of perceiving the world outside the default of despondency.

As enticing as it all sounds, however, we shrink back, convinced of our weakness and tendency to fall short. It doesn't help that the more despondent we become, the more our perspective on prayer is warped. The effort involved in prayer hangs on us like heavy, oppressive scales. Slowly, prayer—and the sense of obligation we attach to it—becomes deadening rather than life-giving, atomizing rather than relational. By the time we take it upon ourselves to question the pit we're falling into, we've been sapped of what little strength we had to care in the first place.

One reason prayer conjures up heaviness within us is that we forget what it is—and what it isn't. We forget that it is not a "should" or an "ought"; it is life itself. It is the medium by which we reawaken the unity between soul and body, God and man, that so easily fragments. Henri Nouwen expressed it beautifully:

> Prayer connects my mind with my heart, my will with my
> passions, my brain with my belly. Prayer is the way to let
> the life-giving Spirit of God penetrate all the corners of my
> being. Prayer is the divine instrument of my wholeness,
> unity, and inner peace. Without prayer, we begin to disinte-
> grate—fall out of integration with ourselves, our neighbor,
> and God.[83]

This chapter commences Part II of this book, which is devoted to practical measures of combating despondency in various corners of our lives. We begin in this chapter with general reflections on prayer—why it takes such a beating in despondency and how we can approach it with a new vision. These meditations are intended to be read in preparation for Chapter 6, which focuses on a specific way of praying during seasons of despondency.

WHY BEGIN WITH PRAYER?

In the original draft of this book, I saved all talk of prayer for last. I envisioned kicking off this more practically oriented section of the book with simpler antidotes to despondency (see Chapter 7) that relate to peripheral areas of life. Deep down, I believe this was an attempt to sidestep my own inadequacy on this topic. When it comes to prayer, I feel like a congenitally blind person trying to fathom a sunrise: I long for the beauty yet unseen. But when I have clients who are struggling to finish their writing projects, I often tell them to begin with the hardest thing first—to start where they are most afraid rather than cowering in the closet of what is easy and uneventful. We could spend our entire lives spinning our wheels on the uneventful, avoiding whatever failure or challenge we are most afraid of.

When it comes to prayer, I feel like a congenitally blind person trying to fathom a sunrise: I long for the beauty yet unseen.

Prayer is like writing. We assure ourselves we'll get to it later, when we have the time or when we've gotten everything else in our lives under control. But prayer isn't something we work up to once we've superficially perfected ourselves. So here I am—prayerfully challenged and all. However arduous it may be, I know of no stronger foundation for anything than prayer itself. The words of St. Paul to the Philippians come to mind:

> Be anxious for nothing, but in *everything* by prayer and
> supplication, with thanksgiving, let your requests be made
> known to God; and the peace of God, which surpasses all
> understanding, will guard your hearts and minds through
> Christ Jesus. (Phil. 4:6–7, emphasis mine)

It seems unlikely that our battle against despondency falls outside
the bounds of the "everything" Paul speaks of. Elaborating on the
theme of "everything" are the words of St. Theophan the Recluse:

> To do everything in the Name of the Lord means to turn
> all to His glory. [. . .] It means also to surround every deed
> by prayer to Him; to begin it with prayer and to end it with
> prayer; as we begin, to ask His blessing; as we proceed,
> to beg His help; and as we finish, to give Him thanks for
> accomplishing His work in us and through us.[84]

This "everything" of prayer envelops our battle against despondency. Let us thus begin in prayer; let us start where the soil has
grown parched. It needn't concern us that we will lose our way
from time to time, or that prayer will on occasion seem strained.
Sometimes a degree of distance in prayer is natural, the inevitable
growing pains of a relationship between two independent beings,
ourselves and God. At other times, however, we create unnatural
distance, shrinking back from God out of shame or fear. These
can be profound moments, since they have the potential to teach
us to stand before God without pride and self-delusion. "The
moment you reach rock bottom, the moment you are aware of
your utter dispossession of all things, then you are on the fringe
of the kingdom of God."[85]

Despondency is understood by the Fathers first and foremost

as a lack of ascetic effort. Speaking for myself, it is often the fear of failure that drives this—I'm afraid of *actually* trying and coming up short (whatever that means), so I only half try and thus don't mind when my efforts slowly fizzle out. Theodore Roosevelt's maxim is something to keep mind: "There is no effort without error and shortcoming."[86] It's not a question of whether we will fall short but when.

To give anything our best—most of all prayer—means facing our inadequacy. It means facing the reality that our attempts will be messier and more circuitous than we'd like to think. Also, it means accepting that prayer does not boil down to some black-and-white measurement of success versus failure—love, after all, keeps no record of wrongs (1 Cor. 13:5, NIV). If anything, success (if it can be called that) in prayer, as in any relationship, is about coming back after we've screwed up, and continuing to come back. "The love of many will grow cold. But he who endures to the end shall be saved" (Matt. 24:12–13). It matters less that we manage everything perfectly and more that we keep on in our pursuit of the Kingdom, despite the temptation to throw in the towel. St. John of Karpathos says to rise again (and again), no matter how many mistakes we've made:

> Even if you fall a thousand times [. . .], rise up again each
> time, and keep on doing so until the day of your death. For
> it is written "If a righteous man falls seven times"—that is,
> repeatedly throughout his life—seven times shall he "rise
> again" (Prov 24:16 LXX). So long as you hold fast, with
> tears and prayer [. . .] you will be counted among those who
> stand upright, even though you fall again and again. [. . .] It
> is more serious to lose hope than to sin.[87]

> ∿
>
> *"Even if you fall a thousand times, rise up again."*
>
> —St. John of Karpathos
>
> ∿

Technically speaking, that last sentence about hope comes from the subsequent paragraph, introducing a new thought. Yet I've always read it as a continuation of the theme of rising again, of the need to cling to hope time after time and misstep after misstep. Giving in to the seeming despair of one's condition is worse than whatever else a person can do, because in hopelessness we turn our back on the Holy Spirit, indeed on the entire promise of salvation. On the other hand, each time we rise again from our struggles and shortcomings, we actualize the Resurrection of Christ in our lives—we move from the cross of our own weakness into newness of life, reencountering the risen Lord.

PRAYER: DOING AND BEING

Prayer is like a coin with two sides, doing and being. The "doing" of prayer includes all the externalities—the words we articulate (audibly or not), the candles we light, the prostrations we make, the spaces we designate for prayer. In Orthodox Christianity, we have an abundance of highly developed rituals and practices to help us cultivate the journey inward. We sometimes burn incense, or use prayer ropes, or set certain corners of our homes apart for prayer. These rituals are not meant to be rote or mindless, but to nourish reverence and to remind us that we are incarnational beings—our bodies must learn to pray as well as our minds.

Within this tradition, learned prayers—lifted from the Psalms or other portions of Scripture—are usually favored over spontaneous ones. Either way, however, a priest I know is fond of reminding his parishioners that prayer isn't merely something one says—uttering words from a book (or our own minds) is not what makes something a prayer. Think of it this way: we can say prayers without praying, and we can pray without saying prayers. "The power is not in the words," St. Theophan wrote, "but in the thoughts and feelings."[88] Are our thoughts and feelings warm and soft toward God, or cold and brittle?

The other side of the coin is "being" in prayer. This is the deeper, interior mode of prayer. Most often, this is experienced as "becoming" rather than simply being; prayer is the expression of our relationship with God, and relationships are continuously unfolding. St. John of the Ladder describes the words of prayer as vehicles that help us "confine [our] mind[s]."[89] They—along with the other "doing" components of prayer—function as a bridge, helping us cross the turbulent stream of our own minds toward dwelling in the presence of God.

This is not to say we ever fully arrive at the other side—quoting St. Isaac the Syrian, Bishop Ignatii reminds us that "there is scarcely a single person who attains to the mystery fulfilled in pure prayer and who, by the grace and love of God, reaches the other side of the Jordan."[90] But we keep stepping out further and further in faith. Without the stepping stones of word and action bringing us closer to the presence of God, we would be left on our own to swim against the current of our thoughts. In short, most of us need to *do* prayer to *become* prayer.

Despondency attacks both the doing and being modes of prayer in different ways. It begins by denigrating the doing, by drawing our attention to corners we could cut. Even if we still pray regularly, we may minimize prayer in other ways: hastening the words of the Our Father, mumbling the Psalms instead of articulating them clearly.[91] These kinds of shortcuts may not amount to much on their own, but over time they cultivate a distinct minimalism or carelessness.[92] It is not merely that we say fewer words or take fewer minutes to complete our prayers, but that on a more fundamental level we begin to offer less of ourselves to God—we stay in our minds before Him, rather than venturing into our hearts. Ultimately, we risk forsaking prayer altogether.

I don't like my prayer rule, but I do love it. It leads me outside the city gates of my fleeting concerns to meet with God. I need the doing of prayer if I am ever to encounter those precious few moments of being.

"A despondent monk," wrote Evagrius, "is dilatory at prayer. / And at times, he does not / speak the words of the prayer at all. / [. . .] The despondent monk never, at any time / performs / the work of God with care."[93] Mumbling, rushing, skipping formal times of prayer entirely—it's all okay, despondency tells us, since it's what's on the inside that counts. Such thoughts, while rooted in a kernel of truth, lead us further down the path of minimalism, a path that St. Theophan explicitly cautioned against: we cannot bypass the "exterior stages" of prayer and "pass directly into contemplation"—most of us simply aren't ready for that and may never be. Instead, "everything must be done in its own time. At the beginning, there is only seed, which afterward develops [. . .] into one form of life or another. Gradualness is necessary."[94]

I appreciate St. Theophan's honesty on this point. Personally, I can't wake up in the morning and just *be* with the Lord Almighty,

Creator of Heaven and Earth. Even if caffeine is factored into the equation, my mind is not naturally inclined toward Him but instead toward memories and complaints and to-do-list items.

In the early days of my Orthodoxy, my spiritual father assigned me a rule of prayer—a modest daily practice. At the time, the phrase "prayer rule" sounded deliciously, liturgically romantic to me. I quickly discovered there is nothing exciting about a prayer rule—no dazzling surprises, no warm fuzzies, no soft Gregorian chant greets me from Beyond when I step into the prayer corner. There is only showing up, standing before God, day after day, praying more or less the same old words whether I feel like it or not.

I barely know what it means to pray, but I do know that somehow all this sameness is good for me—it confronts me, more than anything else has, with the extent of my despondency, that insistent voice within me that would rather be doing anything other than crying out to God. Likewise, prayer pulls me beyond the despondency. All those verses and Psalms—ever the same and yet ever renewing—they lead me outside the city gates of my apathy to meet with God. Sometimes I near those gates, most often I don't, but either way I need the doing of prayer if I am ever to encounter those precious few moments of being. As infrequent as such encounters are, I side with the Psalmist on this: "Better is one day in Your courts / than a thousand elsewhere" (Ps. 84:10, NIV).

Here the discussion loops back to time. Through the eyes of prayer, time is not measured quantitatively but qualitatively. Similar to the two aspects of prayer, time has two modes: chronos and kairos (see Chapter 2). The doing mode of prayer is akin to the ordinary time of chronos. Like the ticking of a clock, "doing"

Like the ticking of a clock, "doing" prayer times and rituals can grow stale—even when we are trying to go beyond the rote motions. But what we are really doing is marking time, catching it as it unfolds moment by moment, and offering it back to Christ.

prayer times and rituals can grow stale—even when we are trying to go beyond the rote motions. But what we are really doing is marking time, catching it as it unfolds moment by moment, and then offering it back to Christ. Every now and then, a twinkling of eternity penetrates the chronos of it all—a moment of being interrupts the doing. We mark chronos so we may be watchful for those moments of kairotic connection, when God finds us anew—or when we find Him. Likewise, we mark prayer by doing, so that gradually, we may learn to be.

PRAYER: MONOLOGUE OR DIALOGUE?

When we begin to show up for the doing of prayer, despondency pushes back. Whereas before, we neglected the "doing" of prayer, we now gravitate away from the "being" of prayer. We may say some words, light some stuff, do some crosses, but we're not actually there, and we don't care to be. In many ways, this is the harder and more destructive face of despondency because it is more deceptive. We're doing nothing less than what we're supposed to be doing—but also nothing more. (As a caveat, there are instances when going through the motions is truly the best we have to offer to God. But there are other times when we camp out in the complacency of empty actions.)

I'm of the opinion that beneath the carelessness is fear—specifically, the fear of being vulnerable, of being truly known by God. When we humans fear God, we hide. Like the unfaithful servant, we hide our talent in the ground, fearful of our supposedly hard master (Matt. 25:24–25). By turning the doing of prayer into an end in itself, we find false comfort in actions and rituals. Prayer becomes a monologue with ourselves that shields us from God.

To grasp what I'm talking about with monologuing, think about the interactions of sportscasters on television. Each statement made by one commentator is followed by a non-sequitur response from the other—a remark about Player X's injury from last season elicits from his partner a reference to Team Y's current fumble statistics. Rarely do these reporters appear to fully hear, let alone engage with, one another—their job consists of entertaining, of keeping the conversation going at all costs. Yet it isn't a true conversation; there are no natural pauses or hesitations as each person processes and responds to the other. There are no disagreements or points of confusion. Instead of a real dialogue, the sportscasters carry on two parallel monologues.

It's fine when such a mode of interaction is confined to sports coverage, but sadly it has come to characterize the way many of us engage with the people around us, not to mention with God. We assume we are having conversations and relationships, since we go through the motions of talking, nodding, and responding, but indeed we are stuck inside ourselves, unable to listen or be available to others. If we are not careful, we will monologue our entire way through life and prayer, never taking the risk of opening ourselves up to another person. In following this path, we avoid the potential for the hurt or disappointment others can cause us.

Prayer is a journey out of our lifelong monologue. Henri Nouwen said it better than I can when he wrote that

> converting our unceasing thinking into unceasing prayer
> moves us from a self-centered monologue to a God-
> centered dialogue. To pray unceasingly is to lead all our
> thoughts out of their fearful isolation into a fearless conver-
> sation with God.[95]

In prayer, as in any relationship, monologuing is easier and emotionally safer than truly dialoguing. It also protects us from the uncertainty in our relationship with God: do we have the courage to "count up the sum of" ourselves before God, in the words of Rilke, and let Him "spend" us as He sees fit?[96] If we avail ourselves of the presence of God, who knows what He'll be like or what He'll ask of us—or even if He'll be there at all.

TURNING TOWARD GOD

Sometimes when I start reading about prayer, I get a surge of energy (pride?) and start making Big Plans to overhaul my so-called prayer life. Whether or not I follow through on such plans, these spurts of grandiose thinking are exhausting. Burnout soon follows, and I grow more despondent than ever. For me, at least, inviting prayer into my life happens best on a small scale. There's no need to make a show of it, for God or for myself. All that's needed, most of the time, is to show up—regularly, mundanely, hopefully. The slow, steady art of relationship is something we're all trying to learn in this life. Whether with our fellowman or with God, learning to love is not a sprint but a marathon.

Marriage is teaching me a little bit about prayer and what it means to be in relationship with God. Several months before our wedding, my husband and I were given an article by Dr. Philip Mamalakis on Orthodox pastoral approaches to marriage.[97] Mamalakis depicts the mystery of marriage as a long process of learning to "turn toward" your partner in the small exchanges of everyday life. This term was originally coined by the Gottman Institute, which has isolated causes of marital breakdown through proven, research-based strategies. The Institute has determined that in strong marriages, both partners continuously "turn toward" each other by acknowledging one another all the time in small ways, rather than just once in a while in big, showy gestures:

> "Turning toward" includes making eye contact, simple nods, attending, listening, and engaging responses, which communicate care, respect and love. Turning toward communicates, "I hear you," "I am interested in you," "I am on your side," "I accept you," "I'd like to be with you." The daily communicating in marriage, as bids for connection, are not just about sharing information but about nurturing connection and intimacy.[98]

When my husband and I first read these words, they sounded too easy—if making eye contact and other small gestures were really all it took, this marriage thing was going to be a cinch. Prior to that point, we had been prone to grand displays. (Someday, they will make a major motion picture about the time my husband flew to Europe to propose to me.) For a long time, we assumed that if it didn't involve a candlelit dinner or some wild surprise, it wouldn't mean anything to the other person.

Now, of course, it seems common sense that regular, tiny acts are the glue of any relationship. The small things are also the hardest to be faithful in—it's easier to go *way* out of the way once in a while (buy a big gift, plan an elaborate surprise) than it is to go *a little bit* out of the way all the time. It is in this difficult, beautiful art of turning toward, though, that another person becomes intertwined with your life, your heart, and your routines, little by little. You are fusing yourself to your beloved, one moment of connection at a time.

The language of turning weaves as a leitmotif through the life of faith. The Greek word for repentance (*metanoia*) is formed from the words "change" (*meta*) and "mind" (*noein*). The term paints a picture of the soul turning away or changing directions. Similarly, our English word "conversion" derives from Latin and literally means "to turn around." To repent and be converted (Acts 3:19) means first to turn away from our brokenness and then to turn toward God.

I don't think this journey of turning ever ends—the Christian life is centered on the need to repent and to keep repenting. Indeed, St. John the Baptist's call to repentance in the Judean wilderness (Matt. 3:2) is in the present tense, which in Greek indicates a continuous rather than a completed action. We are not supposed to repent and be done with it, but to *be* repent-*ing*, unceasingly—to be turning and turning and turning toward God, forever.

I don't know how to do this outside of prayer. And prayer may not happen only at the appointed times or in the "official" ways. Maybe (hopefully) it also happens when we see a beautiful flower, or when we look in the face of our neighbor. All these things, I think, are moments of turning toward, at least when we remember to perceive them that way.

But we should be honest: we forget a lot of the time. It's not prayer we forget about—that's always there, in the back of our mind and on our to-do list, nagging us to follow through so we can check it off our list of accomplishments. What we forget about is the turning. And we forget to be repenting because we have already repented. And sometimes (okay, a lot of the time) we forget about God altogether. We remember Him occasionally, as we run to Him on those once-in-a-while days when we are desperate or maybe just when we're having a Type A personality kind of morning. Ordinarily, though, we forsake turning toward Him unless we have the time, energy, or spiritual stamina to go about it in the "best" possible way.

We pass apathetically by a beautiful flower, a ray of sunshine on a cloudy day, a peaceful moment. We are waiting for that Grand Someday when we will have a full five minutes or a half hour or all our powers of concentration. Often, that time never comes, but even if it does, we will still have neglected that first moment when our soul was prompting a heartfelt turn toward Him. Above all else, prayer is the nurturing of a relationship, and relationships are nourished more by tiny gestures given in authenticity and regularity than by infrequent grandiosity.

This is a difficult but vivifying lesson. Difficult, because it reminds us prayer involves an element of effort, just as any relationship does. It warrants repeating: it's easier to go way out of our way for God once in a while—on a feast day, perhaps, or the first week of a fasting season—than to go a little bit out of our way for Him all the time, remembering and turning to Him in the smaller details of life. And yet, this is energizing as well, because if there's any aspect of prayer that will make sense to us in despondency, it's the short-and-steady rather than the excessive-and-unsustainable. Not every prayer has to be a drawn-out candlelit dinner with God that we've planned months in advance—in fact, I don't think prayer ever works that way. In this, the words of St. Theophan are a comfort:

> Just as a man sees another face to face, try thus to stand
> before the Lord, so that your soul is face to face with Him.
> [. . .] There is no need to arrange an introduction between
> [the soul and Him] for they are old acquaintances.[99]

God doesn't want our wooing, He wants our hearts—beat by beat, breath by breath, turn by turn. How similar these turnings of prayer are to the steady press of chronos time. Time, like prayer, unfolds through regular, unadorned junctures. It is in prayer that we learn not only how to reoccupy the present, but more generally how to mark time. It is the way we come to see, gradually and dimly, the life-giving potential of each moment.

CHAPTER 6

Prayers from the Present

I cannot weep but I can pray,
Then let me not despair;
Lord Jesus, save me lest I die,
And hear a wretch's prayer.

—ANNE BRONTË, "DESPONDENCY"

One day when you are so completely low, so profoundly
desperate that you cannot call out of your own soul any
spontaneous wording, you will discover that these words
come up and offer themselves to you as a gift from God, as
a gift of the Church, as a gift of holiness, helping our simple
lack of strength.

—ANTHONY BLOOM, *BEGINNING TO PRAY*

I RECENTLY GOT TOGETHER WITH A FRIEND WHO IS ALSO in the middle of an extended writing project. We bonded over coffee, bagels, and shop talk. Writing, we both agreed, takes a lot of prayer, and we wished we were better at that all-important part of our work.

"Something I do is set an alarm on my phone that goes off at the canonical hours of the day," she said. "It helps me pray in the midst of whatever else I'm doing."

Part of me envied her success in this endeavor. I had tried

something similar for a while, but it never seemed to work.

"I rarely have time to really pray so often during the day," I explained. "I gave it up because I felt like a failure most of the time."

"Oh—I don't always try to do any kind of long prayer," my friend said with a laugh. "A lot of times, all I can do is to silence the alarm. Other times, I do say a short prayer. But even if it's just turning the alarm off, I try to remember God as I press the button. To me, that's better than nothing—it just kind of interrupts my routine and shifts my focus for a second before I return to my work."

Ordinarily, this thought would have grated on my nerves. *Isn't that taking the easy way out?* I would have wondered to myself. But my friend spoke with almost childlike gratitude, as though she treasured these brief turns toward her Creator more than almost anything else. Her sincerity was infectious.

I think Evagrius would have liked what my friend had to say, too. He wouldn't have been crazy about the cappuccinos and treats we were gobbling up, but he would likely have commiserated with us on the benefit of momentary prayers offered in the hustle and bustle of life. In fact, he compiled an entire treatise of such pithy prayers. He called this method of prayer *antirrhetikos* (ἀντιρρητικός), a term that even in the original Greek is a little awkward. In English, it can be translated as "counter-statement" or "refutation." Whatever one chooses to call it (I'll be sticking with the former), Evagrius's treatise instructs praying in short bursts, using short verses or phrases from Scripture to cut off or "talk back"[100] to destructive thoughts.

By exploring this avenue of prayer in more detail, this chapter—not unlike Evagrius's original treatise—is a celebration of the slow and steady. Building on previous discussions of prayer, it reflects on counter-statement as a small but pivotal turn toward God even in the darkest depths of despondency.

COUNTER-STATEMENT: LESS IS MORE

In the prologue to *Antirrhetikos,* Evagrius cites both King David and Jesus as forerunners in the practice of counter-statement prayer. David authored many of the Psalms, the richest repository of antirrhetic statements in all of Scripture, and Christ used biblical verses to cut off the temptations of Satan in the wilderness (Matt. 4:1–11; Luke 4:1–13). Numerous Fathers of the Church endorsed counter-statement, including St. Macarius the Great, St. Macarius the Alexandrian, St. Gregory of Nazianzus, St. Antony, and St. Athanasius.[101]

Evagrius subdivided his treatise into eight sections that correspond to the primary logismoi (see Chapter 1). Each of these sections contains specific thoughts or ideations with which a logismos might plague a person, followed by a counter-statement to refute that thought. For the sake of example, here is one thought–counter-statement sequence from the beginning of the treatise, in the section on gluttony:

> Against the thought that seeks to be filled with food and drink and gives no heed to the harm that springs from filling the belly:

> Having eaten and been filled, pay attention to yourself, lest you forget the Lord your God, who brought you out of the land of Egypt, out of the house of slavery (Deut 6:11–12).[102]

The destructive thought, in this case, concerns the temptation to eat and drink whatever one wants, regardless of the consequences.

"Against" this is the counter-statement, often a single verse or two from Scripture. In this case, the antirrhetic statement reminds us of God, whom we easily forget when we find ourselves fully satiated.

How exactly do counter-statements work to heal us? To answer this question, we must first clarify that this kind of prayer does not intend to initiate a dialogue with destructive thoughts themselves. St. Silouan (among many others) emphasized that talking directly *to* your demons was fruitless at best—few of us have the stature to oppose evil face to face, as Christ did in the desert.[103] Instead, counter-statement engages in what early Christian theologians called "cutting off" (ἀποκοπή, *apokope*) damaging thoughts, halting their destruction by offering a direct refutation of them.

This term reveals a crucial aspect of how mental processes were perceived by the first centuries of Christians. Thoughts—whether good, bad, or neutral—were seen to proceed not in a linear progression but by constantly cutting each other off, not unlike cars switching lanes on a busy highway. For example, the thought may occur to me to go outside and get some exercise, but quickly the notion of some other, more pleasurable pastime cuts it off, and I decide to stay indoors. In conversation, I may begin a sentence on one topic, but another thought interrupts my line of reasoning, and I begin the sentence over again in a new direction.

According to Evagrius, when it comes to passions and virtues, evil thoughts cut off good ones, and good ones cut off evil ones. I picture this process much like braiding a cord—each thought gets covered and turned as we wrap the next thought over it. Our minds are a complex synthesis of many strands. What matters most, believed Evagrius, were the thoughts we give priority to—the thoughts we allow to do the cutting off. If we let the more damaging tendency of our minds hold sway over our hearts, we grow sick and divorce ourselves from communion with God and man. The more we intentionally cut off destructive thoughts by turning toward God, however, the healthier we become.[104] This is the larger context of counter-statement—it is a way of praying that mentally cuts off our worst thoughts and protects our heart from the tyranny of harmful ideas.

Essentially, what happens when we practice this is that we divide our soul into two halves, "one of which comforts and the other [which] is comforted."[105] Part of us is able to rise above and provide consolation in the midst of despondency with the balm of prayer. We deflect discussion and enticement from the offending thought and instead tend to the broken parts of ourselves that need love, healing, and redirection.

We encounter this pattern frequently in the Psalms. Evagrius, for example, points to this passage in particular:

> Why are you so sad, O my soul? And why do you trouble
>   me?
> Hope in God, for I will give thanks to Him.
> My God is the salvation of my countenance. (Ps. 41/42:12)

There is something beautiful and transcendent in our capacity to demonstrate care within ourselves, especially when the situation least warrants it. In my own life, there have been instances that, for one reason or another, have left me completely bereft. Just when I assumed I had nothing left to give, though, a faint voice of comfort trickled out of some inconspicuous crevasse of my soul.

I don't think I'm alone in that, but it still strikes me as a miracle—in my own valleys of shadows—whenever I discover I have comfort and hope left to give.

One of the snares of despondency is to assume that more is always better. We compare ourselves to others, or we read the biography of a saint and somehow get an idea in our minds that we should be praying longer, harder, more intensely. We forsake the virtue of knowing ourselves—and our limitations—and cling instead to our fictional superselves. (We forget, too, that the value of prayer is not in length or breadth but in the heartfelt giving of ourselves to God.)

While some bulwarks of the faith may have had the fortitude to pray for long hours, most of us don't. This is particularly true in the midst of despondency, when we desperately lack stamina and initiative to sustain even modest prayer praxes. We need to remind ourselves, again and again, that less is often more.

Although counter-statement is not intended to replace a more well-developed rule of prayer, it does provide a path of return to God when we find ourselves at our lowest and most feeble—however often that may be. Its power lies in its intentional brevity.[106] The thinking behind counter-statement recognizes that rather than forcing ourselves to pray "a ton" or read the entire Bible in a year, we need to hone the basics of facing and countering our destructive thoughts, of turning to God in the heat of our battles. We do this best by starting with short verses or phrases, learning to wield them and take aim with them as we would a sword.

There is also an aspect of counter-statement that is lively—even sassy. These prayers are quick, punchy, and purposefully confrontational. They carry an energy all their own, helping to reignite the vigor despondency all but stifles. "In place of the promptings of the enemy it puts the consoling, warning, promising words of God, which enable a human being to overcome deadness at the core of his being."[107] In taking aim at our thoughts, we become warriors, the words of Scripture our flaming arrows. We may only be able to summon our inner archer for mere moments, but the outcomes of many wars in history have hinged on a few decisive shots. Archers ready!

The Psalter is the oldest and richest repository of counter-statement–like prayers. For a sort of all-purpose counter-statement, look for simple supplications or verses that express heartfelt need. One of my personal favorites is Psalm 141:8 (142:7): "Bring my soul out of prison / To give thanks to Your name, O Lord." Historically, the most celebrated counter-statement has been Psalm 69(70):1: "O God, make haste to help me." This verse has been used and recommended not only by Evagrius but also by St. John Cassian, Abba Isaac, St. Benedict of Nursia, and many others over the centuries to lift the countenance to prayer. Aside from this, Psalm 102(101) is designated as "a psalm for one suffering from acedia" or despondency. Finally, Psalms 41(42), 69(70), 87(88), and 114(116:1–9) all speak of crying out to God in the midst of restless spiritual torment and thus serve as collections of counter-statements of particular value during despondency.

Reading those psalms and staking out a verse or phrase within them as your own personal counter-statement could help turn the soul out of the cyclical thoughts of dissipation. They speak not only to the depths of despondent existence, but also to God. When we can't quite find a God-ward inclination within ourselves, the Psalms train our soul in that direction.

As powerful and time-honored as the Psalter is, however, a user's manual would be helpful, something to make sense of our condition and quickly point us to what we need. Evagrius's treatise on counter-statement is one such resource (I recommend David Brakke's excellent translation of *Antirrhetikos*).[108] The counter-statements, often retrieved from forgotten nooks and crannies of Scripture, speak with an almost searing relevance to our condition. An added bonus is the precise way Evagrius expresses wayward thoughts. His knack for illuminating thoughts within ourselves that we may scarcely have been aware of helps develop a more neptic vigilance toward assaults that would otherwise fly under the radar.

I say all of this having spent a fair amount of time with *Antirrhetikos*. Admittedly, my first impressions of the text were somewhat less enthusiastic. Indeed, for a long time, I dismissed the humble compilation of prayers as being too "monastic" and rather uptight about lust and eating habits. With time, though, I came to find an unlikely dwelling place in this treatise, and I began to appreciate its relevance outside the walls of the monastery. In reflecting on several select portions of *Antirrhetikos*, I hope to breathe contemporary life into several counter-statements that directly address thoughts of despondency.

WE HAVE NO LASTING CITY

Against the thought that entices us to see the city, my family, and my loved ones there:

For here we have no lasting city, but we are looking for the city that is to come (Heb. 13:14).[109]

In Evagrius's day, desert monks lived in direct tension with the urban centers of late antiquity. Cities represented the family members monks had left behind. Yet cities were also associated with distraction and deviance. Living in the fourth-largest metropolitan area in North America, this is a tension I am painfully familiar with. My own city is an interesting and bittersweet place—full of diversity and delicious ethnic cuisine, yes, but also traffic, long distances, and high housing costs. On the many days when I must fight to hear myself think, it helps to be reminded that we Christians have been struggling to live in the city for millennia—even Christ had to seek refuge from the crowds once in a while.

This struggle came to a head in late antiquity. In those days, cities were synonymous with spiritual decay, luxury, lust, and licentiousness. After Christianity was legalized in the early fourth century, it was no longer necessary to (physically) die for the faith. Monasticism—dying to oneself and to one's city—became the new martyrdom; many pious souls fled to the desert or wilderness, hoping for some long-awaited peace and quiet. But when they got there, the silence was stifling, as Evagrius's thought reminds us (above). The desert monks missed the city and the people they loved there. Maybe this wasn't such a bad desire, except they had taken a vow to remain among their desert brothers (or sisters). And so they found themselves in a field of tension, pulled between the wilderness they had chosen and the city they longed for.

Monastic or not, all of us are called to die—to the world and to ourselves. This is not an easy death, but it's the way to new life. As Metropolitan Anthony (Bloom) of Sourozh wrote, "We cannot live a life of prayer, we cannot go ahead Godwards, unless we are free from possession in order to have two hands to offer and a heart absolutely open."[110]

The life-giving death of the spiritual life is less an extermination or cessation and more an opening up, a relinquishing. Sometimes this requires leaving the figurative cities of our existence, the places and spaces of distraction, convenience, or familiarity. Sometimes it means being homesick—literally, as when life's course takes us far from home, or figuratively, as when our hearts long for the wholeness and peace from above. Whatever death will mean for us personally, to be a Christian means to live out the rich, paradoxical shape of life wrought from death. Christ tells us to love our neighbors as ourselves, but He also asks us not to look backward once we put our hand to the plow (Luke 9:62). There is a time to embrace and a time to refrain (Eccl. 3:5). There will be seasons of joy, but also seasons of abstinence, and they will be heart-wrenching. When God leads us out of the city—through loneliness, a job relocation, an illness that leaves us bedridden— He is teaching us, slowly, to enter the desert of dying, hoping in His goodness.

I am tempted to sugarcoat this somehow, to say that because of the Resurrection of Christ, everything will turn out fine in the end—and there is some truth to that sentiment. I gladly subscribe to T. S. Eliot's proclamation (quoting Julian of Norwich) that, mysteriously, "all shall be well, / and all manner of thing shall be well." But I am equally convinced by the line that precedes that verse: the life we have been given is "a symbol perfected in death."[111]

No one wants to die—figuratively or literally—even if that is the path to new life. Let us face that, let us know and share how difficult death is. Let us acknowledge when we are too bitter to cooperate with God Himself in the deaths we face, small or large. And when we cannot face God in those realities, let us look to Christ, to His Body—the Church. With some frequency, she shows us a simple and temporary path beyond the city walls of life.

In fasting, for example, we part ways with the "loved ones" of the belly, mainly cheese and bacon (and, it bears repeating, bacon). We come to inhabit a kind of seasonal desert, and the lack of easy comforts is meant to be a little difficult. The purpose of this particular desert is not to mortify the flesh but to know the freedom of renunciation so we may turn to God with more of ourselves than before.

At the risk of sounding redundant, when I think of the cities monks fled from in those long-ago centuries, I can't help but compare them to social media. The internet is every bit as crowded and noisy as any city and demands just as much vigilance in the spiritual life. Perhaps we try to leave every now and then in search of peace and quiet, but our thoughts compel us back—we miss our long-distance friends and family, the bustle of the news feed. And before the rooster crows three times, we are swept back into the current of distraction and drama.

"For here we have no lasting city. . . ." One might expect Evagrius to quell these city-oriented longings by praising the desert—he certainly would have had his pick of verses to substantiate that sentiment. Instead, he begins with the human affinity for cities and companionship and directs that love heavenward, to the prototype of all cities, the eternal Kingdom—the city we have not yet seen with our eyes.

It's a thought that must have resonated with his fourth- and fifth-century contemporaries, who bore witness to crumbling urban centers. The Roman Empire—long envisaged by Christians and pagans alike as an unshakable fortress—was disintegrating, and cities were the first places dissenters attacked. Ten years after Evagrius died, Rome was sacked by the Visigoths. St. Augustine's *City of God* was written in the wake of this grief to console Christians and direct their gaze from the "earthly city"—the civilization of this world—toward the eternal city of God, whose inhabitants surrendered the comforts of this world in their love for Christ. Whether they were city- or desert-dwellers, the promise of the eternal Kingdom comforted Christians of this period with a promise that couldn't be threatened, not even as the world around them fell apart at the seams.

It may not be such a bad thing to long for our families and loved ones or the conveniences of communal life. But when such desires prevent us from entering the desert in faith, we risk becoming blind to the eternal city unfolding around us. Evagrius tells us to stay in the desert but heed our city-oriented longing—it is the beginning of our appetite for heaven.

HERE I WILL DWELL

> *Against the thought of listlessness that is eager to find another cell for its dwelling place on the pretext that the first one [. . .] was very foul and full of moisture so that it got all kinds of diseases from it:*
>
> *Here I will dwell, for I have chosen it (Ps. 131:14).*[112]

When I first came across this particular excerpt, I shared it with a friend. She rejected the suggestion that there is spiritual value in a musty cell—mold, she reminded me, can damage a person's lungs. Mold or no, this particular counter-statement speaks with a familiar bluntness, as though it knows me. The histrionic details with which the complainant laments his cell are endearing—probably because they resemble my own knack for highly articulate grumbling. Bearing in mind Evagrius's wider observations of despondent thinking, I doubt the hypothetical cell was actually moldy or disease-inducing—the entire thought hinges on the word "pretext." The mold functions as an excuse of the mind to legitimize its desire to leave. What is being expressed here is the general temptation to forsake what is beneficial for the soul in pursuit of something easier, fresher, or more appealing to the mind.

"Here I will dwell . . ." The first words of the counter-statement hearken back to the need for stability of place (stabilitas loci) discussed in Chapter 4. Foul-smelling caves aside, we have other kinds of cells we long to escape. They are constructed not of rock or mold, but of the unseen threads hemming us into relationships, tasks, expectations, obligations, unmet desires, and routines. Such threads, while not prone to undue moisture, are subject to their own kind of staleness, which tempts us to cross to the other side of the street, where the grass seems always greener and the air always cleaner. We may even be convinced that such a relocation would be the healthy thing to do. After all, a bit of fresh air never did anyone any harm. Yet perhaps the novelty we seek can come by exercising our freedom to stay where we are.

"For I have chosen it." Too often, we equate choice and freedom with abrupt change, forgetting we can also exercise free will by accepting, surrendering, or submitting to our circumstances. In the face of the tedium I long to escape from, I can *choose* to stay. How does choice apply to issues we never had any choice in, like a terminal illness? In such situations, it feels like the doors of free will have been slammed in our faces—not only did we not choose the predicament we are in, but that same predicament leaves us little hope for the future, no illusions to hide behind. It's tempting to assume this decisive counter-statement is irrelevant to such instances.

And yet, it is when I seem to have the least power over life events that I find this verse's assertion of choice to be the most transformative. It is as though, in the absence of any other decisions, the One Choice stands out like a star in the night: Christ Himself. We may not have chosen our disease, we may have no control over its remedy, but we can still choose to remain rather than resist. *"Abide* in Me," Christ beckons us (John 15:4, emphasis mine)—*Stay. Endure. Surrender.* Anyone in the midst of great pain knows it is a thousand times harder to accept this invitation than to give our hearts over to bitterness or despair. To stay with Christ where we are (rather than to seek Him where we are not) requires surrender and longsuffering, both of which move us to choose between Him or hardness of heart. We may not get to select the struggles in our life, but we do get to choose where—or with whom—our hearts will dwell.

Making such a choice can feel daunting. Which is why I am particularly grateful this verse is in the past tense: "I *have* chosen" (emphasis mine). It reminds me that this is something I've already set my mind and heart to, perhaps back when things were clearer or brighter. All I'm doing now is following through, taking the next small step, staying true not only to God but to myself (or at least the best parts of myself).

BEGINNING TO HELP

Against the thought that neglects the labors involved in the service of commandments:

Blessed is the person who begins to help, who depends on hope [Prov. 13:13].[113]

This thought regards the stubborn tendency to refuse commands, particularly those that involve assisting others. Recalcitrance is a common trademark of despondency. For me, it's usually not the idea of helping I find egregious, but the fact that requests for help undermine my sense of control or autonomy. I've noticed, too, that I begrudge helping myself just as much as I do anyone else. I stay up late reading or distracting myself, despite the quiet inner voice requesting me to go to bed so I won't be exhausted the next day. I eat a piece of cake despite the same voice asking me not to, reminding me of my hypoglycemia and the brain fog that will follow me for the next three days. And when the same voice tells me it's time to exercise, I roll my eyes and try to find a couch to sink into. I don't know if loving others begins with learning to love ourselves (I haven't excelled far enough in either direction to be much of an expert), but I do know that when I fail to love others, I am almost always at odds with myself as well.

These selves of ours are likely not what Evagrius had in mind. But Christ's admonishment to love our neighbor as ourselves will fail to make inroads into our hard hearts if we ignore our own basic needs. Thus, we should listen to ourselves—not just our despondent selves, but our helpful and observant selves as well. Speaking of "should," in the self-help industry today, it is common to disparage the ugly "s-h" word. This line of thinking presumes that "should" and its synonyms mask unrealistic expectations or harsh self-talk (e.g., "I should be thinner" or "I should be more bubbly in social situations").

I agree with this in principle, but we also need to recognize that by categorically refusing to "should" on ourselves, we sometimes swing to the opposite extreme: despondent self-sabotage, or refusing to be faithful in perfectly helpful and necessary things we need from ourselves. It's not self-hating to ask myself to go to bed so I don't have to spend the next day in a daze. Following through on these "commands" is about as demanding as helping someone else—our own needs signify our most immediate experience with human infirmity and vulnerability. Even my best self is not self-sufficient—it needs the other parts of myself to get up off the couch and do the laundry once in a while. Over time, if we scorn our interior commands and requests, we learn to let others down along with ourselves.

The counter-statement Evagrius recommends for cutting off recalcitrant thoughts speaks with an almost resurrectional consolation, reminding us of the blessing of beginning. It redirects us from fighting inner stubbornness with counter-stubbornness (a futile tactic, as anyone who has attempted to win an argument by yelling louder than their opponent knows). Instead, it steers us toward the simple sacredness of starting something new, even when it feels as though we are giving up our sense of control. Blessed is the person who *begins* to help. In other words: blessed is the person who stops fighting—with others or himself; blessed is the person who leaves his stupor behind for a moment and acts constructively.

When we start to warm up to this idea, it should hardly sur-

prise us if despondency demands to know the details before giving its assent: Exactly whom are we to help, and why can't they do
it themselves? How long does the helping part need to last, and
will there be a treat afterward? Evagrius's counter-statement will
never satisfy these questions. Indeed, help can assume a variety of
forms and is not easily pinned down by definitions and pointed
answers. On the most basic level, to help is to exercise love, which
in the Christian tradition bears an element of suffering.

In trying to envision the form helping ought to take, we gravitate toward grand, résumé-worthy gestures—volunteering at a
soup kitchen, for example, or a homeless ministry. Personally,
I think Evagrius was talking about the more ordinary, thank-
less varieties of helping, the kinds that are tainted with annoy-
ance and inconvenience. I think he meant saying "yes" instead
of "You're an adult, why can't you do it yourself?" Even harder, I
think, are the times we aren't being explicitly asked to do something. No one asks us, for example, to be civil and patient when
standing in a slow line at the grocery store—but it's undoubtedly
helpful to those around us when we choose to do so. Rilke wrote,
"You have to be so ready to help, so gentle and kind, that you
spoil it."[114] By being so willing to lend a hand, that old despondent
buildup of stubbornness and resistance becomes anticlimactic.

That this counter-statement emphasizes *beginning* to help is
key. In despondency, changing our ways—breaking out of our
apathetic default in any way—can seem overwhelming or even
pointless. Such feelings may indicate just how unaccustomed we
are to helping people. But they may also reflect a warped sense
of inadequacy that persuades us we are incapable of doing any
good or following through. Yet the blessing in this verse doesn't

go to the person who masters the art of helping on the first try, or sticks to this new beginning without fail until the end of his days. It goes to him who begins, regardless of what comes of that beginning.

The emphasis on beginning can be applied to the wider condition of despondency itself: healing comes to the person who begins to wage war in his heart against his logismoi. As much as sin fragments our experiences, one of the more wondrous aspects of being human is that we were created for unity—at the core of our being is a harmonious synergy of body, mind, and spirit. As a result of that unity, when we want to combat something like despondency, it really doesn't matter where we begin but *that* we begin at all. We can start to help almost anywhere, in any small or seemingly insignificant corner of our apathy, and it will send tiny ripple effects through our lives.

Finally, the counter-statement calls us to "depend on hope." Like helping, hoping is a tricky business. The more I come back to this verse in my own life, the more I am convinced that the hope we must depend on has nothing to do with our innate abilities or stamina. Rather, we must cling to the reality that one small gesture—one tiny beginning—is meaningful in its own right, that a mustard seed of help is worth planting, regardless of whether we have a green thumb in this regard. We may fall back into despondency at any moment, and we will eventually fail to live up to the spotless ideal of patience in line at the grocery store. But for now—in this moment—we are beginning to try, and that is beautiful.

CHAPTER 7

Stepping Stones back to the Present

Look: easy and hard things simply do not exist. Life itself is what's hard. And you want to live, don't you? [. . .] You must be a world unto yourself and with your difficult thing in your center. Then, when it's ready, God will enter into your difficult thing. And do you know anywhere else where you and He can meet?

—RAINER MARIA RILKE, "MORNING PRAYER"[115]

That was his cure:

Out to the fields (before Matins), at a run.
Back to the Chapel (at a run) for Matins.
Back to the grapes (at a run)
   hard work
   for the body

   frees the soul.

—LEW WELCH, "ACEDIA,"

RING OF BONE: COLLECTED POEMS

I'M THE LAST PERSON WHO SHOULD BE WRITING a chapter on practical advice. In my life, despondency too often makes its presence known through flagrant negativity, a "deeply rooted cynicism which to every spiritual challenge responds 'what for?' and makes [my] life one tremendous spiritual waste."[116] I'd rather stay in my comfort zone of heady reflection, where I can dream my dreams and not have to step into the arena of actuality. Writing this chapter (which my editor and others assured me was vital) gave me the invitation I didn't know I was waiting for to inch past my attitude problem and partake of practical theology, trying age-old wisdom on for size in my own life.

Even as I have warmed up to certain insights, however, I remain painfully aware of despondency's tendency to scoff at guidance, to paralyze us with acrimony and doubts. Maybe we have tried and given up too many times, maybe we balk at the apparent naivety of simple advice. And as long as we are being completely honest, maybe part of us even prefers the darkness of despondency to the light of healing—it demands less of us and enables our disinterest, for one thing. For another, it simply feels more real and logical given everything we are surrounded by in the world. This chapter is an exploration not only of the "what" and "how" of becoming less despondent, but also the "why": Why bother? Why try? Why risk failing or hoping or putting ourselves out there yet again, only to be disappointed in the end?

Having laid a foundation of prayer in the previous two chapters, we shift toward everyday strategies to mitigate despondency's stranglehold on our lives. Each of the following six sections elaborates on a virtue or discipline recognized for its capacity to counter despondency—humility, patience, gratitude, confession and community, labor and leisure, and humor. A brief note of clarification is warranted on the final items on this list—leisure and humor—which are not part of the standard repertoire of healing virtues one finds in historical or common pastoral writings on despondency. I include them because they have played an unmistakably supportive role in my own journey, and because they are consistent with Orthodox understandings of the human person. Not all of us have the capacity to be monastics—for most of us, the world of workaday routines and social interaction composes the backdrop of our struggle and must therefore be incorporated into the healing process.

In keeping with the practical objectives of this chapter, each section begins with a reflection and ends with a series of "stepping stones," three or four concrete ideas for implementing the strategy at hand. These ideas are merely suggestions, methods I've tried in my own life or gleaned from others. Before we embark, however, allow me to issue a brief cautionary note. It's something I frequently remind myself of whenever trying to make changes in my life: resist the pull to make (or fantasize about making) too many improvements at once. As Evagrius reminds us, healing emerges from doing things "at the proper time and with moderation," not impulsively or excessively.

The reasoning behind this is clear: "For what is exorbitant and unseasonable is of short duration. What is of short duration, is, however, rather harmful than useful."[117] Too much at once and we won't last very long. This advice is relevant to most endeavors, but particularly to matters of despondency. The more times we burn out and give up on ourselves, the more persuasive a despondent worldview becomes. We begin to believe that not only is the world/political events/life in general worthless, but so are we— healing just isn't in the cards for us.

This cycle of overambition and burnout arises in part from mistaken, all-or-nothing assumptions. We assume that if we are ever to come through this mess, we must do so immediately and completely or not at all. Yet what has been said of prayer in the previous few chapters is also true of healing the soul more generally: start with one small corner of despondency, be as faithful as you can be in that one thing, and let whatever goodness comes flow outward on its own. This chapter is full of small corners, but there are others as well—you'll find them in the writings of Evagrius, the desert fathers, and the countless other pastoral theologians of our faith (if copyright law didn't exist, this book would have many more quotations from Metropolitan Anthony of Sourozh, one of my personal favorites).

Eventually, we can come to see our entire life—even the "bad" bits we are ashamed of—as potentially healing. The vast majority of activities in life are ambivalent—neither strictly good nor bad, spiritual nor unspiritual, sacred nor profane, meaningful nor meaningless. It is the time and manner in which we act that creates value. When we learn, however slowly, to act with intention and thanksgiving with whatever raw materials are placed before us, we begin to see that God has been here all along and that healing is a matter of turning toward Him in our struggle rather than inventing a new self. I say all of this largely to take some of the pressure off so we may think more clearly about healing and aim for patient discernment rather than frenetic overhauling.

HUMILITY

In matters of the heart, all good things begin with humility. As I write these words, today happens to be the Monday after the Sunday of the Publican and the Pharisee. According to the Eastern Orthodox lectionary, this Gospel lesson (Luke 18:9–14) is proclaimed four Sundays before the approach of Lent, priming our hearts for the task of repentance. It's the perfect story, I think, for fellow despondents. No matter where I am in the vicissitudes of spiritual lethargy, I can always locate myself in this narrative. At times I'm the Pharisee, relying on my own strength to fight my battles, paying attention to my own heroic deeds and little else. On days like that, my prayer deteriorates into a monologue of self-focus, the spiritual life hollows into a to-do list I can be proud of. Other days, though, I'm a mess, strewn among the ashes and unsure how to rise from my abyss. I have nothing to be proud of and no glory to bring to God or anyone else. I am saved, over and over again, by the feeble prayer of the tax collector that turns my shame into the seeds of humility: "God, be merciful to me a sinner!" (18:13).

Pride will tell us many lies, but in despondency, it will tell us we can heal ourselves. It will tell us to never mind we've been unable to fix ourselves before, all we need is to keep plugging away—one day, we'll crack the code and all this will be behind us. In Sirach, we are told that "pride is the beginning of all sin: he that holdeth it, shall be filled with maledictions, and it shall ruin him in the end" (Sirach 10:15, DRA). To avoid this peril, sometimes we have to confront our pride, stare it smack in the face for a while so we can see what it's concealing.

As much of a sin as pride is, it also functions as a kind of defense mechanism, shielding us from the painful edges of self-awareness. Like worms wriggling under a rock, beneath our pride hide colorful species of powerlessness, inadequacy, and shame. By covering up these groping little monsters, pride gives us an alternative reality—one in which we have control, in which we are self-sufficient and accomplished and strong. I can forget the "infinite poverty" of my own existence in favor of delusional riches.[118]

In my experience, beating the pride out of myself with humiliation tactics doesn't work—as defense mechanisms go, it will only provoke pride to rise up in defense. Instead, when struggling with pride, I can ask myself what am I feeling vulnerable about right now, what am I trying to hide from? Slowly and quietly and painfully, the worms begin to squirm out from under the rock. Facing and owning my shame is the quickest—and most painful—way I know of to dismantle my pride.

In regards to despondency, the defense mechanism of pride tends to blame other people (or things) for our predicament. Humility gives us the facts: we are responsible for our own despondency, and we cannot use other people (or modernity, or digital devices, alas) as excuses for our spiritual condition. Knowingly or not, we are the ones who choose to become (and remain) despondent. Humility, and the vulnerability that accompanies it, is almost excruciating at times, but ultimately it reminds us of the agency and free will we possess even in the hardest times of struggle. We cannot control others—we can hardly even control ourselves—but we can choose to give ourselves over to Christ, the healer of our souls. Slowly, in humility, we can hope to cling less and less to despondency and more and more to the grace of God, which, like the morning light, is perpetually new despite how many dark nights we have known.

As I mentioned before, pride tries to persuade us to heal ourselves. Endlessly frustrated by our condition, we come up with lofty goals and aspirations—*for the future*. Often, the act of articulating these wonderful intentions is gratifying enough that we never get around to the hard work of transformation available to us through Christ and His Church. We eventually fall from our lofty perch of goal-infatuation back into the morass of despair.

As long as this cycle repeats itself, it remains an obstacle in the long-term, one-day-at-a-time journey toward wholeness. Before we "do" anything, we must acknowledge despondency for what it is: not just a "bad habit" to "life hack," but a deeply embedded pattern of the soul that will not be satisfied until we are dead inside. It is imperative that we learn the art of coming to God from within our despondency, opening ourselves up to Him in all our brokenness rather than waiting until our mess has been cleaned up. Oriah Mountain Dreamer, in her poem "The Invitation," articulates something of what God must hope for us in our relationship with Him:

> It doesn't interest me
> > what planets are
> > squaring your moon . . .
> > I want to know
> > if you have touched
> > the center of your own sorrow
> > if you have been opened
> > by life's betrayals
> > or have become shrivelled and closed
> > from fear of further pain.
>
> I want to know if you can sit with pain [. . .] without moving
> > to hide it, or fade it, or fix it. [. . .]
>
> I want to know if you can see Beauty
> > even when it is not pretty
> > every day.

To be with God, as I see it, we must be willing to touch the center of our sorrow (which is also His sorrow) and bear up under the beauty of being alive in Him, tarnished though that beauty may be by our shortcomings. This is a naked, defenseless mode of existence, and our first instinct is to hide. Yet it is the level of encounter Christ extended toward those He healed.

Recall the many exchanges in the Gospel narratives when Christ questioned people about their ailments and the wider sickness of sin in their lives. Anyone who has tried to discuss an embarrassing ailment with a physician has a taste of what these folks endured—we tell our doctor about how tired we've been, but he wants to know how often we've been exercising or eating fatty foods; a Samaritan woman goes to fetch water and Christ wants to know about her infidelity. On a related note, it is striking how many of Christ's miracles were followed by the command to stretch something—a lame hand, a crippled back. To extend any part of the body is to render it more open to attack—physically and emotionally. How scary it must have been to stretch a wilted appendage that for countless years had been the very source of one's shame.

Let's face it: healing is not easy. It's fine if someone (ideally ourselves) can *fix* us, but our pride will sneak to our defense the moment healing threatens the status quo. Healing entails opening rather than closing ourselves, stretching rather than cowering, engaging rather than silencing, surrendering rather than controlling. And it almost always brings our skeletons out of the closet.

This is why we need humility—it's the only way we can access the vulnerability necessary to experience some semblance of healing. Without it, even our best efforts become self-enclosed labors that hinder us from communion with the One who saves. The twelve-step adage is applicable here: admitting you have a problem is the first step to fixing it—and by "problem," we are specifically talking about things we are powerless to remedy by our own, human strength.

Stepping Stones of Humility

» **Be still.** The next time you find yourself in the anxious, self-protective pride of despondency, spend a few moments dwelling in that reality before (or instead of) trying to launch a campaign to fix yourself. Take thirty seconds to read the Psalmist's words aloud slowly, letting each word dwell in your mind: "Be still and know that I am God" (Ps. 45/46:11). *Be still.* Other translations of this verse render the phrase as "be in awe" (46:10, ISV), or "cease *striving*" (46:10, NASB). I particularly love the latter: cease from striving, cease from figuring it all out, cease from blaming or shaming or justifying. And in all of this ceasing, remember—even just for a moment—that God is God, even when we are at our worst.

» **Pray for your enemies.** Praying for our enemies helps to counteract the blaming spirit of despondency. Begin with a line from the morning intercessory prayers included in the *Orthodox Study Bible*: "Save, O Lord, and have mercy upon those who envy and affront me, and do me mischief, and do not let them perish through me, a sinner." Memorize these words or incorporate them into your daily prayers. What makes them so powerful is their acknowledgment that when we have been wronged—or think we have been wronged—our hatred and hostility cause even greater damage.

» **A new litany.** Formulate a list of items or people you tend to blame for the unpleasant things in your life, especially your struggle with despondency. It can include specific people, things, memories, or even technologies. If anything, this may illuminate certain trends to address in your next confession. For now, though, practice letting whatever people are on your list off the hook—even for moments at a time. Use the list as a litany of supplication, praying for each person involved by name: "Save, O Lord, and have mercy on _____, and do not let him/her perish through me, a sinner." When I pray these words, I imagine my hands letting go of the blame I've stockpiled. If the practice seems helpful—that is, if it does anything to dismantle the attitude of pride or blame toward others—consider returning to it periodically. If it intensifies your rage, talk through things with your father confessor or someone else you trust.

PATIENCE & PERSEVERANCE

Patience is a direct counterattack against the restlessness of despondency, which hastens us to the next task before we've completed what we started. Whatever it is that coaxes you away from the cell of what's at hand, Evagrius is adamant we not run in the direction our despondent thoughts urge us:

> You must not abandon the cell in the time of temptations, fashioning excuses seemingly reasonable. Rather, you must remain seated inside, exercise perseverance, and valiantly

welcome all attackers, especially the demon of acedia, who is the most oppressive of all but leaves the soul proven to the highest degree. Fleeing and circumventing such struggles teaches the mind to be unskilled, cowardly, and evasive.[120]

More succinctly, Metropolitan Hierotheos of Nafpaktos says that "[p]ostponing the time of satisfying a thought, helps us to be rid of it."[121] Putting off following through on a temptation drives it away from us.

Patience is hard, I think, because it feels passive. We want to *do* something: slay the dragon, battle our foes, be victorious in the epic battle against the internet or sloth. I have this nagging fear that if I don't *act* in some immediate, grand way against my temptation, I will implode and give in. It is in these types of moments that we begin to encounter a paradoxical truth about patience: we have to be patient with despondency itself. Our first instinct, when the heavy stone of apathy settles in our stomach, is to drop what we're doing and "fix" whatever has broken within us—we'll stop folding the laundry or working and seek out the newest blog post, prayer, or experience that will put an end to the feelings we are having. In many cases, though, our attempts to fix things are simply a more sophisticated form of the same old restlessness that undergirds

༄

Perseverance is the severing of [despondency], the cutting down of thoughts, concern for death, meditation on the cross, fear firmly affixed, beaten gold, legislation for afflictions, a book of thanksgiving, a breastplate of stillness, an armor of ascetic works, a fervent work of excellence, an example of the virtues. —Evagrius[119]

༄

our despondency in the first place. It may seem strange, but the frantic scramble to put an end to despondency is yet another path by which we run from the cells of our lives. The cure is not outside us, but within.

Stepping Stones of Patience

» **Get to know your cell(s).** We have the freedom to dwell in the present—as slow as it feels sometimes—but to do so we need to know what it consists of. What is your cell, the space in your life you are responsible to occupy? You probably have many of them, according to different commitments or times of day: the work cell, the cleaning cell, the writing cell, the evening commute cell. When you find yourself in a cave of sorts that seems confining and intransient, look around. Notice how big it is and the ways you are tempted to exit it (e.g., via grumbling, checking text messages, or sleeping in). Sometimes, just getting more familiar with our cells can be freeing—we begin to see they are not as narrow or boring as we imagined. Take, for example, one of the most confining cells in my own life: the stuck-in-traffic-on-a-crowded-bus cell. I am always trying to inwardly escape or resist this cell, usually by thinking rude and incendiary thoughts about the bus driver and the people around me. When I clench up and try to resist the reality that this is where I am, every stop of the bus and cough of a fellow passenger is torture. When, on the other hand, I look around and take notice of where I am—the people (i.e., human beings made in the image of God) who surround me, the weather outside, the cheerful remark of the bus driver—my surroundings recover a sense of spaciousness. Sometimes just choosing to be where we are makes our cell seem (a tiny bit) more expansive. I can actively decide how I want to inhabit that space and time—I can choose not to give dirty looks, I can choose to say a short prayer for the lady with a cough or listen to a good lecture on my phone. In doing so, we begin to activate the potential for truth and love hidden in these otherwise confining moments.

» **Stay put . . . for two minutes.** When you feel like fleeing your respective cell, agree to stay put for a short period of time— two, five, or ten minutes to start with. Use a timer if necessary. Say to yourself, "I will keep working on the current task for ten minutes and then check my email," or "I will wash dishes for two minutes before watching TV." We can all wait two minutes if we set our minds to it, and putting this little wedge of time between us and our immediate desires creates space for clearer thinking and resolve. It's not that watching TV is necessarily bad for us—what we're trying to combat is the impulsivity and mindlessness that bully us into despondent idleness.

» **Do more things that require patience.** It may sound counterintuitive, but when hastiness and restlessness strike, slow down—*way* down. Read a section of a book, poem, or psalm aloud, slowly, not letting yourself skip over any of the words. Alternatively, take a walk but move at a snail's pace or just stand still and look around. If you look (or sound) ridiculous while trying any of the above, you are doing it correctly. For a few minutes or so, slowing down may make you want to scream. Eventually, though, the insistence of your impatience will break, like a fever. It will likely return soon enough, but you've created a space of relative calm in the present that you can return to in the future.

GRATITUDE

I once attended a talk on mental health and faith given by the late John Bentley Mays, a gifted and well-known journalist in the Toronto area.[122] As well as being a sincere Catholic, Mays suffered from severe depression virtually his entire life. The talk he delivered that night was a humble, honest testimony to the value of resurrectional faith in the bowels of deep depression.[123]

During the question-and-answer session following the talk, someone asked Mays whether he had learned to recognize in himself any harbingers of an impending depression. I expected him to cite one of the many symptoms ordinarily associated with depression—fatigue, irritability, or "the blues," to name a few. But Mays' response caught me off guard: he emphasized instead the loss of gratitude. Just before a major depression struck, he would notice that he had stopped giving thanks for ordinary things in life, like when his wife cooked dinner. He might still feel completely fine in all other ways, but many years of battling depression had taught Mays that for him, a cessation of gratitude was the most consistent forewarning that another storm was on the horizon and he needed to change course.

Although Mays was specifically talking about clinical depression, his realization is worth considering in the context of spiritual vitality and despondency. In both the Old and New Testaments, not to mention classical and patristic wisdom, thanksgiving is associated with health and life. Cicero purportedly described gratitude as the mother of all virtues, and according to St. John of Damascus, it is the preventer and destroyer of despondency (in conjunction with patience).[124]

Why is thanksgiving—and its absence—so powerful? At the risk of sounding clichéd, it's because gratitude comes from the heart, the spiritual center of our being discussed in Chapter 1. We cannot think or rationalize our way into thanksgiving, and history is full of ample accounts of people giving thanks when it made little sense to do so—in concentration camps, for example, or in the midst of terminal illness. Our ability to give thanks is an indication that we are living from the soul outward—that our soul is not being hindered by other components of our being.

I'm of the opinion that the inverse of thanksgiving is not ingratitude but rumination, a relentless mental preoccupation with resolving the unfavorable aspects of our circumstances. Not only is rumination exhausting, it also magnifies the anger and dissatisfaction that underlie despondency. As with Mays and depression, the lack of thanksgiving should be a red flag to us in regard to despondency. Among other things, it suggests we may be living too much in our minds—that our mind is not *dwelling* in our heart, but oppressing it.

It is comforting (if not a bit scandalous) that the Bible rarely commands us to *be* thankful but to *give* thanks. I don't know if there is a linguistic reason for that, but it helps to bring thankfulness down to a practical level. Giving thanks is an action rather than a feeling, and actions are often more finite—and easier to muster—than feelings. I may not be able to be thankful for all of time and eternity, but I can probably manage to give thanks for a second or two for the apple I'm eating or the comfortable chair I'm sitting in. Or I can take a time-out from my frenetic impatience and say thank you to the bagger at the grocery store or the stranger who held the door open for me.

Giving thanks—as opposed to merely being thankful within oneself—is inherently relational: you can only give thanks *to* or *for* someone or something else. As soon as we offer thanks for anything or anyone, we reach outside ourselves. We connect ourselves to the blessings God has surrounded us with. In doing so, we lay hold of a new, transfigured way of being-in-the-world (*Dasein*), one that reveals our basic need for and delight in the grace and mercy of God. Just as our lungs keep breathing, thanksgiving keeps us turning toward God, who alone "gives to all life, breath, and all things" (Acts 17:25). But what are we to give thanks for? I think we assume that gratitude must flow from the big to the small, from global theological truths to the particulars of life, as though it's only through the lens of the Resurrection that we can perceive the seemingly mundane details of our lives—the people, places, and objects that cross our paths—as gifts from God, opportunities to encounter Him.

But I don't think that's how it works. We come to thankfulness the other way around. For me, in the jaws of bitterness and dissatisfaction, I have to take baby steps, giving thanks for what I can see, hear, taste, or smell in the here and now. And I have to remind myself to give thanks *to God*—the giver of all good things—instead of doing so only as an insular intellectual exercise. Perhaps once I have begun to recover some semblance of gratitude, I may inch thanksgiving back to the awesome reality of the Resurrection. Over the course of our lives, we can hope to learn to give thanks for *all* things and at *all* times (1 Thess. 5:18). I love how St. Basil portrays this:

> As thou takest thy seat at table, pray. As thou liftest the loaf, offer thanks to the Giver. When thou sustainest thy bodily weakness with wine, remember Him Who supplies thee with this gift, to make thy heart glad and to comfort thy infirmity. [. . .] As thou art putting on thy tunic, thank the Giver of it. As thou wrappest thy cloak about thee, feel yet greater love to God, Who alike in summer and in winter has given us coverings convenient for us, at once to preserve our life, and to cover what is unseemly. Is the day done? Give thanks to Him Who has given us the sun for our daily work, and has provided for us a fire to light up the night, and to serve the rest of the needs of life. [. . .] When thou lookest up to heaven and gazest at the beauty of the stars, pray to the Lord of the visible world; pray to God the Arch-artificer of the universe, Who in wisdom hath made them all. When thou seest all nature sunk in sleep, then again worship Him Who gives us even against our wills release from the continuous strain of toil, and by a short refreshment restores us once again to the vigour of our strength. [. . .] Thus wilt thou pray without ceasing; if thou prayest not only in words, but unitest thyself to God through all the course of life and so thy life be made one ceaseless and uninterrupted prayer.[125]

Every moment in life offers an opportunity to pause and give thanks to God. This is such a beautiful thought that we may be tempted to leave thanksgiving to the poets—or a particularly skilled Byzantine homiletician like St. Basil. But don't be fooled: thanksgiving is not an intricate art form, it's a plain and simple choice, one we decide either for or against at every moment. Sometimes, thanksgiving happens all on its own, trickling up like a forgotten spring through the cracks of our hearts, but for most of us veteran despondents, it's a searing battle.

Stepping Stones of Thanksgiving

» **Pray the Akathist of Thanksgiving.** Consider incorporating the Akathist of Thanksgiving (also known as "Glory to Thee") into your daily routine, perhaps by reading through it one or more verses per day alongside other devotional practices you may have. You could also recite single phrases spontaneously throughout the day, counter-statement style (see Chapter 6), whenever you find yourself hemmed in by a particularly dark cloud of thanklessness. If you are unfamiliar with this service, it is a stirring expression of thanksgiving that was written against the backdrop of World War I and the Russian Revolution. The full text is widely available online free of charge.

» **Give thanks for three things.** As you lie in bed at night, give thanks to God for three things that happened during your day, whether monumental or trivial. You don't need to *feel* thankful—the point is to cultivate not a heightened emotional state but a calm awareness of the goodness God gives us so we can offer it back to Him. Putting words to our thanksgiving activates the faculties of our perception. If it seems awkward to say something so informal as "Thank You, God, for _____," consider borrowing the phraseology from the Akathist of Thanksgiving: "Glory to You, O God, for _____" or "Glory to

You, O God, for giving/showing/granting/allowing/
being _____."

» **"Thankswriting."** If you (like me) are prone to sleep or
anxiety the moment your head hits the pillow, consider what
I call "thankswriting." I have a small journal devoted only
to thanksgiving. Before turning out the light, I try to list
one or two items per day using the same phrasing as above.
Somehow, writing these statements rather than just saying or
thinking them helps my mind focus on the task at hand—one
to three phrases or simple bullet points will do. The added
benefit of this strategy is that on days when I'm having a
particularly difficult time giving thanks, I can reread previous
entries, which in and of itself becomes something to give
thanks for.

» **Use "Glory to God" as a frequent prayer.** After using one of
the above stepping stones for a while, you may find yourself
wanting to bring thanksgiving into the rest of your day. I
find the simple phrase "Glory to God" is a helpful place to
begin. Whether spoken in our minds or quietly aloud, it gives
a vocabulary for thanksgiving so we don't have to reinvent
the wheel every time we want to turn to God in gratitude.
So when a pomegranate is unusually easy to peel, when you
finally finish washing the dishes in the sink, when you trip
but don't get hurt: Glory to God. I have said before that it is
not necessary to feel a certain way—and it isn't—but don't be
surprised if a quiet sort of joy occurs organically. Give thanks
for that, too, but don't cling to it or despair when it ebbs and
flows. Glory to God!

CONFESSION & COMMUNITY

I once asked a physician friend what the hardest part about being a doctor was. His response has stuck with me through the years: "Being upfront with people," he said. "It's hard telling people the truth sometimes, and it can also be hard hearing the truth from my patients." Doctors are perhaps the only folks left in our society with the authority to be completely, ruthlessly honest. They have our implied consent to ask pointed questions, to make judgments and diagnoses, to declare that there is something in us that needs to change. As sobering as such pronouncements may be, they are often crucial for healing. To fix a problem, you must first face that problem for what it is—in all its shame, embarrassment, and frustration.

In spiritual matters, the practice of repentance is the first step in admitting we have a problem. True repentance re-turns, or reorients, us away from our sin and back toward God. As humans, however, we prefer the theory rather than the practice of repentance. Surrendering our shame to God means relinquishing the sense of control we think we have over our lives, global events, or other people's ability to hurt us. To perpetuate a feeling of autonomy and control, we resort to "problem solving" our sins (or those of others), determining how we screwed up and how we can avoid doing so in the future, without ever turning to God or reconciling ourselves to others. Although this may resemble repentance from a distance, it is sometimes little more than a thinly disguised form of rumination, a frantic effort to change and fix rather than face and encounter. When healthy self-awareness becomes warped into a circuitous preoccupation with our own inadequacies, we grow entrenched in despondent thought patterns.

The myth of control that surrounds our sinful tendencies is often more difficult to surrender than the sins themselves. But that's what repentance asks of us: total surrender, total reorientation. The surrender I'm describing is not self-diminishing but self-actualizing—when we relinquish the jagged edges we have clung to for so long, we free ourselves to cooperate with Christ. Our hands and hearts become open to receive love and life. For Evagrius, repentance was closely tied to the sacrament of reconciliation (also called confession), which in turn was bound up with community and relationship. We cannot do confession on our own—we need another to hear us and have mercy.

The sacrament of confession the Orthodox Church now follows has evolved over the centuries. In the early Church, it was commonly an act that took place before one's entire local community of believers, since repentance reconciles us not only to God but to one another. For logistical and other reasons, this soon became less common, and the sacrament gradually developed into our current practice of confessing one's sins to God in the presence of a spiritual father, who not only prays for us but also counsels us in our struggle. Still, reconciliation stands at the heart of how confession is understood in Orthodoxy—just as sin cuts us off from community (with God and man), so in repentance and confession are we grafted back into that community. This process, as Evagrius saw it, was a vital step toward healing—it gives us the opportunity not only to truly face our sin, but to let it go and be reconciled to both God and man. It is the outward sign of the inward journey of repentance that opens us back up to God, to life, and to love. Essentially, it means throwing our brokenness into the abyss of God's love, which, like a sea, "has no bounds and is immeasurable" (St. John Chrysostom).

The relational context of confession reminds us how vital it is to cultivate fruitful community in the midst of despondency, which continually pulls us toward isolationism. Despondency "is rebuffed by community life," St. John Climacus observed.[126] Investing in meaningful connections provides an alternative to the truncated interactions that occur when we impulsively use others as instruments to rescue us from our loneliness. What stands at the heart of healthy, fellowship-minded relationships is a willingness on our part to love others in truth and in love, as Christ loved us—without impulsivity, controlling others, or a desire to satisfy ourselves at all costs.

Stepping Stones of Confession and Community

» **Participate in community.** One way to strengthen your involvement in community and fellowship is to ask your priest if there are any ministry needs in your parish, such as organizing a food pantry or visiting shut-ins. Alternatively: what are your interests or areas of expertise? Do you enjoy chess, baking, storytelling, writing, knitting, walking, genealogy, books, civic engagement, movies, service, hiking, or something else? Join a local group that is devoted to an area you already enjoy or would like to know more about—a local knitting circle, for example, or a genealogical society. (If you're at a loss, search the groups available in your area on meetup.com.) Once you find a suitable parish or community group, decide on a level of commitment that is manageable in the long term and stick to it—community cohesion is about showing up even when we may not feel like it.

» **Initiate community.** Another way to cultivate community is to create it. Connect with someone you haven't heard from in a while, host a dinner party, or volunteer for coffee hour at your parish. Another, more systematic strategy is to look over your list of interests from the previous bullet point and figure out how to turn one into a communal activity. Then, start small: open it up to a few friends or family members. Recently, for example, my husband and I started a regular board game night in our apartment—whoever is free to join us brings a game or a snack to share. It's small and easy, but one way to bring people together in a meaningful and hopefully uplifting way.

» **Confession is medicine.** "Fight[ing] the good fight" (1 Tim. 6:12) against despondency requires taking confession seriously. Prior to my becoming Orthodox, confession, to me at least, meant writing in my journal or calling a friend. As beneficial as these activities were (and continue to be), they can easily turn into little more than an emotional rant. In the Church, however, confession is afforded the sanctity of a sacrament—we believe that God is active in the raw elements of our confession and the priest's prayers of absolution. Because of that, the Church teaches us to treat confession with sobriety, respect, and humility. It is easy simply to go through the motions or find little shortcuts here and there. Think of sin as a serious medical condition and confession as one of the recommended treatments for it. How would this change the way you approach confession? You would find a doctor you can trust, first and foremost—in this case, a spiritual father. And just as you would for a medical consultation, you would prepare yourself ahead of time, compiling a record of symptoms and questions. Basically, you'd go into such an appointment as if your life depended on it. We should approach confession with a similar degree of focus and concern—it is only in exposing our illness to Christ, the physician and healer of our souls, in the presence of others that we can be made whole.

LABOR & LEISURE

Labor is central to the human condition—as is our (typically) antagonistic relationship toward it. Prior to the fall of Adam and Eve, work was tied to meaning and beauty—man's task was to tend the Garden, the material manifestation of God's goodness (Gen. 2:15). Work wasn't "necessary"—according to St. John Chrysostom, the Garden brought forth fruit without being tilled, and work was an exercise of the enjoyment and freedom God bestowed on humanity.[128]

After sin entered the world, the earth no longer bore fruit without labor. Work became necessary for survival, since it was now only through sweat and toil that Adam could procure his daily bread (Gen. 3:19). Our experience of work is distinctly touched by the postlapsarian condition. Much to the chagrin of our ego, work of any kind reminds us that we have needs, that we cannot subsist as totally independent and autonomous beings. The necessity

Let the rising sun find in your hands a book, And after the second hour, your work.
—Evagrius[127]

of labor also confronts us with the reality of death, the awareness of our mortality. Bearing this in mind, it seems only natural to "thank God it's Friday" and be ever hankering for the next evening, the next weekend, the next vacation, the next interval of freedom from responsibility.

Flying in the face of our modern-day, vacation-craving instincts, however, ascetical theology regards work—particularly light manual labor—as a source of healing from despondency. Among other things, work occupies the mind so it doesn't tyrannize the soul:

> [T]he thoughts [of the mind] bring to the soul their opposing activity whenever they catch it unoccupied with godly considerations. Therefore, do the work of manual tasks for the love of humanity and the work of the rational mind for the sake of the love of wisdom, in order that on the one hand there may be hospitality for guests and a consuming fire for laziness, and on the other hand a guide to contemplation and a winnowing of thoughts.[129]

Work that is good for the soul is hard enough that the mind must focus on it, but easy enough that the work can be sustained for long periods of time. The desert fathers, for example, supported themselves by weaving baskets. There is something beautiful in this peaceful, steady work—even for those of us who can't quite manage to fuse work with active prayer as they did. To me, basket-making symbolizes the redemptive undertones of simple, everyday tasks. There is a humble creativity in performing ordinary tasks like making the bed or folding clothes—jobs that must be redone day after monotonous day and that fail to amount to anything momentous in the end. Yet such tasks are intensely creational—they bring a new layer of order and beauty into the world we inhabit. When we can manage such tasks with even a hint of grace and care, they are transfigured into something holy.

I've always found it touching that after Christ had risen from the grave, He apparently stopped to fold the grave cloth that had once covered His head (John 20:7). Pious traditions abound as to the fate of this cloth—some believe it was the famed *Mandylion*, the so-called "Icon Made Without Hands." Conjectures aside, my eyes well up a bit whenever I remember that Christ allowed His Resurrection to be transmitted through this simple, sullied piece of linen; we are told that when Christ's followers saw this folded cloth, they knew His body had been resurrected, not merely stolen or moved. It's unclear why this strip of fabric would have that effect—perhaps Christ had a signature way of folding things, or maybe it dawned on everyone that a grave robber wouldn't stop to tidy up a stray piece of linen. In any case, if something so *ordinary* (and ritually unclean) as this section of used grave linen had its own perfect time—its own encounter with the resurrected Christ—then no task or object is truly void of potential in the grand scheme of our salvation. Think about it: the first thing Christ did upon His ascent out of Hades was to fold some laundry. I try to store this in my heart for the seasons of staleness, the times when ordinary tasks pile up and keep me from more "exciting" activities.

We all need clothes to fold or baskets to weave—tasks that give us an occasion to redeem the ordinary. How can we bring this quiet sense of purpose into the various forms of work we engage in throughout the day? Evagrius recommends setting a small goal that can be accomplished in one sitting and refusing to rise from that task until it is finished. Human beings crave purpose—having even a basic target to aim for imbues our activities with a teleological, ends-oriented significance.

When I am hired as a writing consultant, part of my job entails helping authors get "unstuck" in the writing process. I often have to remind them—and myself—that it is better to meet small goals consistently than to set more ambitious ones and burn out. It is better to write for fifteen minutes a day over time than to try writing eight hours for one day and give up the next. Grandiose expectations are exhausting and often unprofitable in the end. Chronically sabotaging our own intentions makes us lose trust in ourselves, which ultimately fuels more despondency.

Proceeding in a slow, steady fashion from one manageable goal to the next, Evagrius recommends working as much of the day as possible, stopping only for prayer (and, one assumes, bodily needs). Of course, outside a monastery we can interpret this idea in a more multifaceted way, but his general point is this: people are better off working (and praying) than remaining idle. Although contrary to our leisure-loving sensibilities, this has been affirmed by a number of psychologists, particularly Mihaly Csikszentmihalyi. While working, our minds focus on a single task and enter what Csikszentmihalyi calls the state of "flow," when we become "completely involved in an activity for its own sake. The ego falls away. Time flies. Every action, movement, and thought follows inevitably from the previous one, like playing jazz. Your whole being is involved, and you're using your skills to the utmost."[130]

In ascetical theology, this single-minded, ego-quieting focus is viewed not as an end in itself but as a step on the path toward a more prayerful life. A millennium and a half ago, St. Basil addressed the need to balance prayer (*theoria*) with good works (*philanthropia*).[131] St. Benedict later expanded on this idea; his famous Rule is frequently summed up with the Latin motto *ora et labora* (pray and work), a mantra that resounded throughout Western monasticism in the Middle Ages. It's a phrase that reminds us, first, that prayer itself is a kind of work. Moreover, work and prayer are complementary, not antithetical, activities: life consists of both prayer *and* work, not of prayer *or* work, nor of prayer *despite* work. The more we hold work and prayer in tandem, the more each transfigures our experience of the other. Praying and working our way through life, we stand with one foot on earth and one in heaven—creatures who partake of both time and eternity.

Part of shifting our perception of labor depends on nurturing a more meaningful practice of leisure. St. Augustine of Hippo actively cultivated periods of "sanctified free time" (*otium sanctum*). Whereas worldly otium, or leisure, consists of idleness and dissipation, otium sanctum finds its rest in the contemplation of Scripture. Augustine believed that nourishing restful spaces in our busy lives is necessary for the soul and body to be more attuned to the Word of God. He most often used his free time to study and meditate upon Scripture, which provided a quiet counterpoint to the active way of serving the poor and loving one's neighbor. Ss. Gregory and John Cassian similarly affirmed the need for rest within the Christian life.[132] Long-term spiritual growth is sustained by balancing activity with restful contemplation.

There is a famous story about St. Anthony the Great, a third-century desert father who himself struggled with boredom and despondency, in which a visitor was scandalized to find him relaxing with his fellow monks. After his guest chastised him for playing rather than praying, Anthony found a bow and arrow and asked the visitor to pull the string back as far as he could. As soon as the visitor complied with his wishes, Anthony asked him to draw the bow even more taut. The story continues until the visitor admitted the bowstring was too tight—if he pulled it any farther, it would snap. St. Anthony responded that it is the same with the work of God—we will break if we stretch ourselves too much. It is necessary to counter spiritual effort with relaxation.

The call for rest is hard to square with despondency, which is so often experienced as laziness and lethargy. In such cases, it seems, too *much* rest is the problem. Yet, as Dylan Pahman writes, "It would be more accurate to say [. . .] that [despondency] causes laziness than that it is laziness."[133] I would add that perhaps laziness itself doesn't consist of excessive rest but is instead a symptom of a broken, fallen form of rest. Just as sin alters our stance toward work, so it warps our experience of rest, mainly by obscuring the fact that godly rest, too, is a kind of work—it is meant to serve a redemptive purpose. God's rest on the seventh day wasn't the cessation of all activity—He was active, blessing and sanctifying the seventh day and beholding His creation. Likewise, when Christ lay in the tomb (also on the seventh day of the week, the Jewish Sabbath), He was harrowing Hades. In His rest, He refashioned or re-created creation in the shape of the Resurrection.

Bearing this in mind, we could endeavor to infuse (at least some of) our own rest time with redemptive, re-creational elements.

At the very least, we should remember that the purpose of rest is to reenliven ourselves—to fill and be filled with new life. I don't know about you, but "vegging out"— relaxing as it is—does not leave me feeling more alive afterward. In fact, I usually feel more disengaged and apathetic than before. On the other hand, other activities, such as knitting or repotting my houseplants, leave me with a renewed sense of vitality, even if they require more mental and physical energy than binge-watching the latest period drama.

In my own life, I am trying to work toward these more re-creative activities, my own version of otium sanctum. Sometimes it is not just a matter of sheer willpower—the "mind-over-matter" approach doesn't work if I am truly burned out, physically or mentally. Like prayer, my appetite (or lack thereof) for holy free time is a litmus test of my stress level, as well as my overall spiritual and emotional health.

Shifting our approach to work and leisure is an attempt to recover the life humanity knew in the Garden. Even something as simple as setting a minor goal or working quietly on a peaceful pastime asserts our free choice and thus allows us to relate to work via freedom and enjoyment rather than fatalism or mortality. Both labor and leisure become avenues of reengaging with the present moment and the life God has given us.

Stepping Stones of Labor and Leisure

» **Set a goal.** For one day or week, intentionally practice setting clear goals throughout your work day. Remember that ideally those goals should be small and something we can accomplish in one sitting (e.g., in the two hours between my coffee break

and lunch, I will contact the first five clients on my list). If
your work consists of tasks others assign to you, setting a goal
could mean intentionally taking on those tasks out of your
own volition and setting them aside for single-minded focus.
Alternatively, you can set a time-specific goal concerning
your attitude while working (e.g., "For the next hour, I will
not cooperate with bitter thoughts about my boss," or "From
now until my break, I will smile and say hello to everyone who
comes into the office—even the cranky delivery person").

» **Take a break (or five).** One way to bring a more wakeful,
neptic attitude into our work is to take frequent, short breaks
to recenter ourselves. I use the so-called Pomodoro method
when I work—I have a timer that goes off every half hour or
forty-five minutes, and I try to at least stand up, take a deep
breath, and walk around for five minutes—it gets my blood
moving, helps my eyes relax, and gives my brain time to
process whatever I'm doing. Work-related tasks can suck us
into a narrow perspective; regular breaks keep our heart and
mind fresh and alert.

» **Find a basket.** Find your own version of the early monastic
practice of basket-weaving. Many of us already have these
types of activities built into our day in the form of cleaning
or cooking. Bringing a new sense of purpose to one of these
tasks helps us recover a more life-giving attitude toward both
work and rest. In finding a basket, what you're looking for
is a simple, manual (involving the hands) activity to which
you can bring a greater sense of vigilance and thankfulness.
At first, don't focus too much on the thoughts you may have
while engaging in said task—instead, try approaching it with a

bit more thanksgiving (remembering one needn't *feel* thankful to *give* thanks). Let the satisfaction of completing a task fill you as much as it can. Over time, you may want to add an element of prayer to your activity. You could start with a short phrase from the Psalms (we discussed many in Chapter 6) or the Jesus prayer. I have to say that in my personal experience, the tasks that work best for this are highly repetitive—I've already mentioned knitting, but I would put swimming laps in the same category, as well as walking and chopping vegetables. These tasks involve repetitive body movements over a long period of time, which help vivify the mind and redirect it to the heart. In the course of writing this, I asked numerous individuals what activities in their daily life facilitate this kind of attitude. Here are some of the things they mentioned:

- Knitting, crocheting, cross-stitch
- Ironing, hanging laundry
- Chopping vegetables
- Shoveling snow, raking leaves
- Washing dishes
- Making the bed
- Drawing
- Writing icons
- Making pottery
- Chopping wood
- Mowing the lawn
- Walking
- Sewing
- Gardening, watering houseplants
- Mopping floors

- Kneading bread dough
- Making prayer ropes
- Polishing or dusting things

Interestingly, one person responded to my query that she actually does weave baskets, and that this pastime is every bit as ripe for prayer as the desert fathers make it out to be. Perhaps we need to revive the practice!

» **Choose your rest.** This is the part where I tell you to quit your Netflix subscription and delete your Facebook profile forever. Just kidding! What might be more realistic is to develop a list of activities that are both restful and re-creational rather than mindless. Once in a while, when you feel you need a rest, try to participate in one of these activities before (or instead of) hitting up the couch. You could aim for once a day, but if this seems particularly daunting, try instead for once a week. Before I was married, Sunday afternoons were my re-creational time—every week, I gave myself the goal of finding beauty. I'd take a walk or go to an art museum and try to find one thing that really caught my eye—an early-blooming flower, Breton's depiction of light, the façade of a historical building. Sometimes I'd write a poem about it or take a picture, but most of the time I just tried for a few moments to appreciate that thing and give thanks to God for it before moving on.

HUMOR

The virtue of humor is likely among the last items one would expect to find in a book on despondency—which is why I've saved it, literally, for the end of this book. (That was my idea of a joke.) Lame witticisms aside, humor helps us recover the vitality despondency robs us of.

Several years ago, I listened to a talk by Kallistos Ware.[134] I have long been mesmerized by Ware's ability to season even the driest topics (medieval scholasticism comes to mind) with knee-slapping jokes. In this particular talk, he reflected on his personal philosophy of humor, which, as he sees it, enables us to let our defenses down. Simultaneously, laughter causes an upsurge of energy within us. Riding on the wings of laughter, our soul can jump up through the cracks of our defenses and grab hold of ideas we would otherwise reject or overlook. This is why a joke sometimes succeeds in communicating a point that would otherwise fall on deaf ears. (I distinctly recall a class I was teaching in which my students were having trouble understanding—and spelling—"gnosticism," despite my best lecture maneuvers. I resorted to referring to the ancient heresy as "*gnot* your grandma's Christology." By the next test, the students had largely mastered the material, not to mention grown pretty tired of my lame puns. "By the way, your jokes are *gnot* very funny," wrote one student at the end of an otherwise well-framed essay response. I was pleased.) Kind, well-timed humor is a gift from God that can benefit our struggle against despondency. I'm reminded that a common synonym for *fun* is *light*, as in "to make light of something." Wise humor—the kind of humor we need in despondency—draws light out of the darkness; it reveals love and truth rather than undermining it.

One specific mode of humor is especially helpful in addressing despondency: the ability to tease ourselves or our situation in a loving way (I said *tease*, not *berate* or *harass*). Self-reflexive humor serves the dual purpose of nurturing humility on the one hand and providing alternative means to address despondent tendencies on the other. David Athey, in his essay "The Theological Necessity for Humor," points out that one often finds this form of humor alive and well among the saints of history. The many stories attributed to the desert fathers, for example, are thinly disguised jokes. These anecdotes manifest the playful humility through which these holy men saw themselves:

> Did you hear the one about holy Abbot Moses? When he ran into some pilgrims who were coming to see him, the Abbot refused to act important and said of himself, "What do you want with him? The man is a fool and heretic!"[135]

As Athey sees it, this attitude is one we would do well to emulate. "If we do not laugh at ourselves and allow others to laugh at and with us," he explains, "we tend to worship ourselves. Making fun of ourselves is like making a good confession."

Adopting a more playful attitude toward ourselves and our shortcomings pulls us out of despondent thinking more swiftly than any other approach. It's not a permanent solution, of course, but even a few seconds' smile is enough to get our foot in the door of our own mind and start to redirect it toward the heart. Sometimes when I'm particularly frustrated with myself or life in general, I'll spontaneously recite some inane tongue twister as fast as I can. Other times, I'll leaf through a folder filled with pictures I've collected of me making funny faces—they always make me laugh. It lightens the mood enough to enable me to step back from the heaviness in my heart.

Next time your passions dial your number, try teasing rather than conquering them. My personal favorite strategy is to make up a nickname for my despondency—ideally something silly and Seussian—and refuse to refer to it by any other name (off the top of my head: the lazy pooch, the frumpy sloth). Rather than wallowing in the dark, all-encompassing cloud of despondency, we can instead say to ourselves, "Does that frumpy sloth think I'm going to leave my cell in the middle of my work?" Or, "Here comes the lazy pooch again."

According to certain saints and theologians of the Church, it's usually detrimental to full-on *dialogue* with our passions— we wouldn't strike up a whole conversation with our despondency. Nonetheless, attaching a moniker to our arch-nemesis in the third person helps activate our power of recognition while also detracting from the power of despondency. It reminds us we are distinct from our thoughts and can hold sway over them. And if some good old-fashioned teasing is enough to sidetrack my destructive thoughts for a moment, those thoughts probably weren't as controlling as they initially felt. Despondency can be a bully, but it does not have to defeat us.

All of this amounts to understanding humor as one more path back to the present moment. Jokes and silliness summon us to perceive and appreciate reality as it is, with all its ironies, quirks, and contradictions. In doing so, we begin to see there are other facets of our circumstances than irritation or cynicism. By its very nature, humor always gives us an alternative perspective: any good joke involves the element of surprise, a reversal of our expectations. At the same time, humor conjures inside of us an energy to relate, to move beyond the stupor of dejected isolationism.

I'm reminded of a fascinating belief Aristotle held that human beings become "ensouled" the precise moment they laugh out loud for the first time as babies.[136] As he saw it, laughter produces a current of warm air that fuses the soul to the body. As much as this view clashes with Christian anthropology, there is beauty to be found in his understanding of things: even Aristotle ("chief grumpy pants himself," a friend commented) could appreciate laughter as an intensely connective, integrating act.

Yet it is not always easy to laugh or crack a joke—it requires a great deal of creativity, especially from the gloomy valleys of despondency. Plus, what if our jokes are just *"gnot* funny," as my student unabashedly asserted? Regardless of the difficulties and risks, when we avoid humor altogether, we adopt a hollow, darker shade of existence. Quoting again from Athey's essay: "If we kill the laughter in our lives, some rough beast will rise up to fill the void. God spared Laughter (Isaac) and provided another sacrifice. The ram, a symbol of war, was burned up in Isaac's place."[137] Despondency is one of the demons that will sneak in to occupy the vacuum of humorlessness—always ready to suffocate whatever joy is to be found in the present, always ready to suck us into anxious worries and feeble perceptions.

Finally, humor helps us to learn vigilance. It teaches us to watch and wait for something greater—the punchline, the end of the joke, the reason behind it all. The next time you are at a dinner party and someone begins telling a funny story, look around and observe people as they listen. Likely, you will find them leaning forward, their eyes dancing in hopeful expectation: everyone wants to be ready for the punchline. In fact, the bliss of *waiting* for the punchline of a good joke is almost as enjoyable as the joke itself—I'm often unable to hold back the floodgate of my laughter until the punchline, I'm so easily caught up by the teller's sheer animation.

How similar that awakened, expectant attitude is to the vigilance Christ encouraged His followers to adopt. We are called not just to wait around for Him but to do so with eager, even happy anticipation. Most of the time, spiritual vigilance seems like a chore—like the disciples in the Garden of Gethsemane, we easily grow fatigued and disheartened. The Resurrection was the biggest punchline of all—the ultimate irony. If we learn to wait—with joy and expectation—we may find Christ's presence already leaking in anticipation out of the seams of our realities.

As I've already alluded to, jokes are one of the most powerful teaching tools in the world. When I taught medieval history, I could not help noticing my students did not share my enthusiasm for the finer details of eighth-century political reforms. The only exception to this trend was when I managed to turn something into a joke, hardly difficult given all the funny names back then (side note: my apologies to any Dagoberts or Charles the Balds who may be reading this). Some of my jokes fell flat, but my students did learn the names of Charlemagne and his sons. Maybe this is because humor has a way of creating space in our narrow, cyclical apathy—it's the fastest (and funnest) way to jam a stick in the spokes of insistent carelessness. Wise humor chisels a crack in despondency just wide enough for our souls to slip through, get some fresh air, and see the bigger picture.

Stepping Stones of Humor

» **"A nasty wasty skunk."** Read, sing along, or listen to the song "You're a mean one, Mr. Grinch," but replace all mention of "Mr. Grinch" with the word "despondency." Call me a five-year-old, but it's impossible to make it through that song without at least a mild grin. When despondency has really got me in a stupor, I'll occasionally mutter some strange lyric to myself: "Your heart is full of unwashed socks, right now," or "You really are a heel." It's exactly the kind of admonishment I need to hear sometimes.

» **Improvise.** Think about attending an improv comedy class or workshop—or at least a show. Along with being hilarious, improvisational comedy is based on the so-called "Yes, and . . ." approach. According to this methodology, all participants agree to accept the scenario at hand and build on it, rather than negating or disregarding it. This understanding directly counteracts the energy of our egos, which tends to say no or turn away out of pride or fear. As it teaches us to manage our egos in simple, comedic games, improv can profoundly affect our behavior and outlook in other areas of life. Bonus feature: since you need other people to improvise *with*, this stepping stone doubles as a way to foster community and triples as a form of re-creation.

» **Play.** Speaking of recreation, one important form of leisure *and* humor is relearning how to play, something we adults easily forget how to do. Playing is defined by three basic criteria: first, it has to be an activity that brings you pleasure;

second, it should be the tiniest bit silly, lighthearted, or imaginative; third, it can't have an intended outcome—you can't play to achieve something like a prize or higher status. What are some examples of play? I, for one, am still a big fan of the old-fashioned swing set (I am that adult who will run across the playground in the middle of a walk, to my husband's embarrassment). Luckily, there are plenty of more socially acceptable forms of play: card games, riddles, crossword puzzles, playing pranks on family members (proceed at one's own risk), dancing, reading comic strips, playing Mad Libs, making up a skit, for example. A group of friends I once had would meet once a week during the summers and read through famous plays, each of us taking a part or two—it was, literally, playful. The beauty of play is that it gets us out of our heads, where despondency lives. It may not get us straight into the heart, but it takes us about halfway there, which is closer than we usually are.

CONCLUSION: WHERE TO BEGIN?

These are a few places where I think we can begin to reclaim our lives from the wilderness of despondency—I hope they have been helpful. The question now is where do we start? It seems too menial to start with something small, but if we start with every-thing, we will exhaust ourselves and wind up deeper in the same slough as before. I'm reminded that one of the most beautiful things about sacredness is that it's not all or nothing—it comes to us in small, ordinary things and times, and asks us to see the holy in finite moments. For whatever reason, we humans can only understand or encounter holiness in small morsels at a time—

in a Chalice, a piece of bread, a sip of wine. Any encounter with the sacred reminds us that it is enough to start somewhere, any-where—it is enough to put one foot forward, to turn to Christ for one real moment. Wherever we begin, Real Life will seep out into other areas of our existence.

Lately I have been thinking a lot about this and the implica-tions it has for spiritual endeavors. Sacredness is not unilateral, as we perhaps assume. It is the token of relationship—between God and man, temporal and eternal, cosmic and earthly. It is, there-fore, a two-way street or a stream with two sources. On the one hand is Christ, who makes objects holy by imbuing them with His presence. On the other hand is humanity—we must also par-ticipate in sanctifying things for them to become holy. In biblical understandings, the main way we do so is to set those things—times, objects, activities, or thoughts—apart from other things. The Holy Chalice, for example, is sacred not only because it has housed the presence of the Lord, but because we continue to devote it and offer it to God for that purpose. By setting the Chal-ice apart, we are saying to God that this great gift of the Eucha-rist is special to us. Over time, the Chalice comes to represent not only the Eucharist itself, but also our ongoing synergy or coop-eration with Christ, our continual and appreciative "Yes" to His presence.

Virtually anything can become holy when we cooperate with God in and through it. When we say we are going to give thanks to God for one thing every day, or we are going to pay more atten-tion to the beauty of God's creation, or we are going to seek out a spiritual father, what we are really doing is setting that one endeavor apart from the rest of our chaotic, despondent way of being. We are agreeing that we will say "yes" to God in that one thing. We are devoting ourselves to a single-minded purpose and joining ourselves to the activity of Christ in that purpose.

If you don't know where to start, start somewhere—whatever place you choose will be sacred, not because it is the "right" or "only" place to begin, but because whatever we do toward "the least of these," we do unto Christ (Matt. 25:40). No gesture—no matter how small—is trivial when it is done in the simplicity of care and love.

Re-Presenting Reality

Home is where one starts from. As we grow older
The world becomes stranger, the pattern more complicated
Of dead and living. Not the intense moment
Isolated, with no before and after,
But a lifetime burning in every moment.

—T. S. ELIOT, "EAST COKER V" FROM *FOUR QUARTETS*

FOR MUCH OF MY LIFE, THE PRESENT MOMENT WAS A gaping blind spot. Whatever hope was to be found in the Christian life was tied to either the past or the future—to the first and second advents of Christ, respectively. Rarely did hope arise from the here and now, from the actual shape of lived experience. As a result, the steady press of time seemed like an unyielding holding pattern, forever dissociating me on the one hand from the acts of Christ, now more than two millennia old, and from the eventual prospect of eternal life on the other. Since it is only in the present moment we can encounter Christ, faith seemed less like a real experience and more like an intellectual exercise.

It was a deliberate choice, then, that the subtitle of this book express the need to regain the present in faith and life. To find the present is to find the risen Lord. This reengagement with the particularities of time and circumstance at each juncture of our lives cultivates a spirituality full of living encounters and experiences rather than ossified events and disconnected beliefs. By way of conclusion, I would like to depart from the heavier theme of despondency and look to the newness of life that awaits us—not in the hereafter, but in the here and now.

✻ ✻ ✻

I BARELY REMEMBER THE EASTER SUNDAYS of my childhood, at least not the Resurrection part. We went to church, we learned about the Resurrection, but in my mind is a vacant space where all those cheery sunrise services are supposed to be. What I do remember are the Maundy Thursday dramas I attended in high school and college.

On the eve of Good Friday every year, my church put on a passion play. We'd show up and quietly find seats, our otherwise cheery and well-lit church building now submerged in dark, reflective silence. On an elevated platform at the front of the nave sat a banquet table that was sparsely set with chalices, matzo, and bitter herbs—the makings of a Passover meal. Slowly, a motley collection of fellow parishioners filed onstage, now transformed in costume and countenance into first-century peasants and fishermen.

We watched the familiar scenes unfold: Christ washing His disciples' feet, indignant Peter protesting this incomprehensible role-reversal, Judas receiving from Jesus a morsel of dipped bread. And then there was the Garden of Gethsemane, the fervent prayers, and the betrayal. Last of all was the Crucifixion, sometimes so graphically depicted I had to avert my eyes. As the stage darkened around Christ's final words ("It is finished"), the pastor stood to preach about Christ's saving death, about how the Crucifixion was the most painful way a person could die in the first century, and how this was necessary to atone for our sins. It was the same series of events year after year, and we took it all in with solemn reverence—we were not there to be entertained, we were there to remember and to worship and to be filled.

And I *was* filled—with many things, I suppose, but also with a haunting kind of emptiness. No matter how much I tried to find myself in the events onstage, there was always a disconnect. I never felt a part of the narrative, not even the times I got to act in the play myself, clamoring among an angry mob for Christ to be crucified. There it was, year after year, salvation unfolding before my eyes. But it was always at a distance—not just spatially, but temporally. The ragged costumes, the peppery perfume of vinegar and herbs, the carefully scripted lines—everything was so believable, yet so far from ordinary experience. I couldn't shake the feeling that I was watching the spiritual equivalent of a Civil War reenactment. In their fervent attempt to make historical events more realistic, these passion plays underscored the sense that the saving acts of Christ were just that: historical events.

Slowly, the same disconnect began to tinge the waters of my entire life. At the time, I was barely soldiering on through what felt like more than my fair share of grief. Everywhere I looked, salvation seemed to have passed me by. Hymn after endless hymn proclaimed that Christ *was* risen (past tense). The occasional communion services I knew were performed strictly in *remembrance* of Christ. Any hope I had of the Resurrection breaking into my current circumstances required clinging to the past or future poles of Christ's entrance into this world—whatever He was up to in the here and now was only tangentially related to what He did on the Cross so long ago.

For a long time, I assumed this was simply how faith worked. The prophetic writings and psalms of the Old Testament, after all, were awash in the memories of God's acts of old, depicted as indications that He would act again, someday, by sending His Messiah to rescue Israel. But it slowly dawned on me that we Christians knew the Messiah, and we knew He had conquered death. We knew that in His body, time and space and eternity had converged. *Doesn't that change things?* I wondered. A God bound by the past (or future) no longer enticed me—I longed to know what St. Paul meant when he said, "Behold, now *is* the accepted time; behold, now *is* the day of salvation" (2 Cor. 6:2).

Fast-forward a scant handful of years. By the time I came across the writings of Fr. Alexander Schmemann, I had already begun to taste a new flavor of time and faith in the form of the Orthodox Church. I had already stood through the long but rich services of Holy Week; I had already noticed the emphasis on the present tense in Orthodox worship. "This is the day of Resurrection," we proclaimed—not just once a year on Pascha, but seemingly all the time. The Resurrection was everywhere—even something as simple as standing up from a kneeling prayer was understood as a type of Christ's rising again. And all of this—the Resurrection, the present-ness—had begun to shape me in ways I could not explain at the time. Whatever suffering I faced was no longer meaningless or chaotic, it was a part of the story—a story that ends not with a cross but with an empty tomb.

In the works of Fr. Schmemann, I found expression for a new, present-oriented vision of Christianity. He believed that Christians are called not to commemorate the Resurrection, as though it were (only) a historical event, but to re-present it—to make

Christ present among us as a living fact.[138] Representation, as he understands it, is a form of work the Church is eternally engaged in, a reality we are perpetually realizing. When I first considered Schmemann's view of things, I imagined the Church was caught in some cosmic game of tug-of-war, stretched between the past and future of salvation. As each new moment unfolds in real time, we give an old heave-ho, reaching back in salvific history and dragging the Resurrection with all our might up to our present moment. *Re-presenting.*

Slowly, though, that comical picture dissolved into something new, and probably closer to Schmemann's intended meaning. As I see it now, it's not we who occupy the present, but the resurrected Christ, who in redeeming fallen man also redeemed the emptiness of time by filling it with Himself. It is not that Christ just happens to dwell in the present—the present moment is the present moment precisely *because* Christ dwells there. He endows it with form and content, meaning and potential—and love. Likewise, we live in the present only inasmuch as we abide in His presence.

Carrying this line of thought still further, it is not the Resurrection we are trying to maneuver—dragging it through history to the time at hand—but our inner selves. We are continually reaching and pulling our minds up through the strata of dissipation, dejection, and despondency and into encounter with Christ. As hard as this effort may be for us, it at least does not require period-appropriate costumes or lengthy drama rehearsals to replicate. The historical particularities of Christ's life—real and important as they are—are not ends in themselves but a beginning. They transmit to us the narrative arc that continues to reverberate through all of creation: first life, then death, and finally newness of life; cross, tomb, resurrection; creation, sin, reconciliation. To re-present Christ's life is to live out this pattern (or type) of reality, to progress with love for God and man through every painful cross, harrowing descent, and joyful resurrection we experience on this earthly sojourn.[139]

All of this has profound implications for the way we view spiritual sickness and healing. It means that despondency, for example, is in a certain sense not real. It has no substance of its own but is rather a distortion of the Real, an impaired vision of Christ's victory over death. Here I am reminded of what happened to Saul after his encounter with the risen Lord en route to Damascus: he lost his ability to see. After three days in the dark whale of blindness, "there fell from his eyes *something* like scales, and he received his sight at once; and he arose and was baptized" (Acts 9:18). Somehow, standing face to face with the Christ of the Resurrection prompted a hard, opaque crust to obscure Saul's vision of reality. Was he blinded by the bright light Christ radiated, or by the shame and vulnerability of standing before the very Person he had persecuted?

Adam and Eve, fearing a chance encounter with the Lord after their sin, fashioned clothes of fig leaves to cover their nakedness (Gen. 3:7). Likewise, Saul's eyes—in a sort of psychosomatic desperation—fashioned a covering of scales. And we? We find other, more invisible artifices to hide behind—apathy, procrastination, distraction, despair—which are no less blinding to the heart than the loss of physical vision is to the eyes. Of course, when we are in the depths of the miry pit, despondency feels every bit as real and immediate as the Resurrection, indeed usually more so. But in the light of Christ, who has lovingly filled all things—even hell itself—despondency is little more than a hardened scale, a scab we perpetually manufacture to numb the risk of encountering and being encountered by the risen Son of God.

In a world that has been refashioned in the shape of the Resurrection, what does it mean to be healed? It means, in a sense, that we have already been healed—that is, the Resurrection has already changed us. This is not to minimize the pain of our struggle, but rather to remind us that regeneration is not altogether foreign or antithetical to our being, however broken things may seem through the scales. Receiving healing means returning to our most basic and essential selves, and continuing to return, over and over again, a thousand times each day.

In fact, this repetitive return to being is the essence of liturgical worship. The liturgies of the Orthodox Church are punctuated countless times by a simple supplication: "Lord, have mercy." To modern ears, such a prayer may sound stifling and self-diminishing: is God really so vengeful we must beg His forbearance at every turn? But in Orthodox conceptions, mercy is the balm of salvation, and to ask it of God affirms that He is merciful and loving in the first place. In fact, to make any deep request of anyone is to stand naked and defenseless before that person. We will pray "Lord, have mercy" hundreds of thousands of times over the course of our lives, because that's how many times it takes to relearn how to stand that way before our Creator. Redundant as it seems, worship in the liturgy turns time into a pilgrimage back—not back to our shame and feebleness, but through our feebleness and back to engagement, back to communion, back to Christ, one *Kyrie eleison* at a time.

In another sense, healing is not a matter of gaining something new but of letting go of what has been distorted—having the courage to allow the scales to fall from our eyes so we may see and be seen by the Lover of our souls. As humans, it is our instinct to grasp and cling and clench; we hold our breath when doing something difficult, we store up memories we'd rather forget, we hire expensive massage therapists to dissolve the tension our muscles refuse to surrender. To let go of our scales and shackles is to face our lack of control and certainty. This is hardly an easy or automatic response to the ordinary pain of living—which is why we need the help of one another and the stepping stones of pastoral wisdom. "Spiritual disciplines such as praying, fasting, and caring help us to return home," Henri Nouwen once wrote. "As we walk home we often realize how long the way is. But let us not be discouraged. Jesus walks and speaks to us on the road. When we listen carefully we discover that we are already home while on the way."[140] Even when we are still stuck in our solitary sloughs of despond, Christ is in our midst, raising us up just as He Himself is raised up.

When we proclaim the Resurrection of Christ, we ultimately declare His *presence,* which is eternally sustaining and elevating all of creation. We proclaim the blueprint that all reality conforms to in its visible and invisible properties—existence brought forth from nothing, fullness wrought from emptiness, order hewn from chaos, life borne out of death. Even if, in our frailty, some of our scales persist for a time, let us have the courage to profess with St. Paul that *today* is the day of salvation—not two thousand years ago, not happily ever after in heaven, not when we finally manage to get ourselves sorted out, but today. And in ten years, it will still be today. And every year and day and moment hereafter, from now until "the last syllable of recorded time,"[141] it will still be the today of salvation.

What we are really saying is that the Resurrection is right here, right now—*life* is now; *self-emptying love* is now; *hope* is now. And all these "nows" will continue to continue unto the ages of ages. This is the present moment that is our gift from God, bestowed upon us not just once two millennia ago, but every moment. This is what we lose when we retreat into the slow, apathetic death of despondency. And this—all of this—is what we stand to regain when we turn toward home and let the scales fall from our eyes.

> *I do not count myself to have apprehended; but one thing I do, forgetting those things which are behind and reaching forward to those things which are ahead, I press toward the goal for the prize of the upward call of God in Christ Jesus.*
>
> (PHIL. 3:13–14)

Discussion Guide

INTRODUCTION

1. In the introduction, Nicole talks about an early experience she had with despondency. Do you remember moments of despondency as a child?

2. Who were the Mrs. Ds in your life, the folks who brought demons out into the healing light of conversation and honest struggle?

3. How can you be a Mrs. D to someone else?

4. How does despondency relate to our experience of time?

5. What are some ways the carelessness of despondency surfaces in your life?

6. At the close of the introduction, Nicole describes this book as an exercise in facing demons as co-suffering members of Christ's Body. What demons are you facing in your life? How can we struggle together in a meaningful, Christ-centered way?

CHAPTER 1

1. How would you define despondency in your own words?

2. How does despondency relate to care, pain, and distraction?

3. What are the dangers of medicalizing spiritual conditions and spiritualizing medical conditions?

4. What is meant by the "soul-centered paradigm" of early Christian theologians?

5. How does seeing sin as a sickness rather than a crime shape our attitude toward despondency?

6. This book is based on the idea that despondency is the most temporal of the passions. What is meant by this?

7. In what arenas of your life do you most struggle with despondency?

CHAPTER 2

1. Are time and eternity separate realms? What implications does this question have for the rest of our lives?

2. In the introduction to this chapter, Nicole points out that eternal life begins when we start to exercise our capacity to realize life as we live it. How do you think this vocation of "realizing life" counteracts despondency?

3. How do time and eternity both reflect God? What is the difference between kairos and chronos? Can all of time be understood as eternal love in action?

4. How does the fallenness of sin affect our perceptions and experiences of time? How does time make relationship, love, and free will possible? Could we have these things without time?

5. In the last section of Chapter 2 ("Time and Transformation"), Nicole describes time as the giver of second chances. What does she mean by that?

6. Staniloae wrote that "eternity is life and life is movement." We don't often think of eternity as a realm of movement, life, and change. Should we reconsider?

CHAPTER 3

1. This book is based on the idea that despondency is the most temporal passion and is rooted in a broken relationship to the perception of time. In what ways do you see this playing out in your life?

2. What is the present moment? Why is it so important in the context of despondency?

3. How is time characterized by both fullness and emptiness?

CHAPTER 4

1. What does the monk's cell represent outside monastic life? How is the present moment like a cell? What are the different types of cells we flee to?

2. What is the relationship between inner emotions and thoughts and the external symptoms of despondency?

3. What are the physical, spiritual, and mental ways you escape the present?

CHAPTER 5

1. What are the two modes of prayer, and how do they mutually reinforce one another?

2. How does despondency attack the doing and being of prayer?

3. What is meant by monologuing and dialoguing? How do you see these tendencies play out in real life?

4. What is "turning toward"? How does it tie together the overarching themes of this chapter: prayer, relationship, time, and despondency?

CHAPTER 6

1. What is counter-statement, and what value does it have in regard to despondency?

2. What does it mean to "talk back" to our destructive thoughts? What are the benefits and dangers of talking back?

3. What does the "city" represent to you? What deserts has God called you into, now or in the past? What have you learned there?

4. What would stability of place (*stabilitas loci*) look like nowadays? Does this virtue serve a purpose anymore?

5. What are the commandments or people that are hardest to serve? Where can you begin to help?

CHAPTER 7

1. How does cynicism play out in your life? How do self-doubt and burnout get in the way of healing?

2. Why is it important to start small when making changes in your life?

3. Which "stepping stone" did you find most useful? What would it mean to implement this in your life?

4. At the end of the chapter is a discussion on sacredness. How do our efforts become sanctified? How is it that holiness is a two-way street? Does this change your perspective on despondency or the spiritual life?

5. Where will you begin?

Bibliography

Amis, Robin, *A Different Christianity: Early Christian Esotericism and Modern Thought* (Albany, NY: State University of New York Press, 2003).

Art of Prayer, The: An Orthodox Anthology, ed. Igumen Charion Kadloubovsky, trans. E. and E.M. Palmer (New York: Faber and Faber, 1997).

Athey, David, "The Theological Necessity for Humor," https://incommunion.org/2004/12/12/the-theological-necessity-for-humor/.

Berry, Wendell, *This Day: Collected & New Sabbath Poems* (Berkeley, CA: Counterpoint, 2013).

Bloom, Metropolitan Anthony of Sourozh, *Beginning to Pray* (New York: Paulist Press, 1970).

Bradshaw, David, "A Christian Approach to the Philosophy of Time," http://www.uky.edu/~dbradsh/papers/Christian%20 Approach%20to%20Phil%20of%20Time.pdf.

Bunge, Gabriel, *Despondency: the Spiritual Teaching of Evagrius Ponticus on Acedia,* trans. Anthony P. Gythiel (Crestwood, NY: St. Vladimir's Seminary Press, 2011).

Bunyan, John, *The Pilgrim's Progress,* ed. Roger Sharrock (Harmondsworth: Penguin Books, 1965).

Conquering Depression: Heavenly Wisdom from God-Illumined Teachers (Platina, CA: St. Herman Press, 1995).

Cullman, Oscar, *Christ and Time: The Primitive Christian Conception of Time* (Lousville, KY: Westminster John Knox Press, 1964).

Demakis, John G, "Historical Precedents for Synergia: Combining Medicine, Diakonia and Sacrament in Byzantine Times," in *Raising Lazarus: Integral Healing in Orthodox Christianity,* ed.

Stephen Muse (Boston: Holy Cross Orthodox Press, 2004), pp. 13–22.

Dysinger, Luke, *Psalmody and Prayer in the Writing of Evagrius Ponticus* (Oxford: Oxford University Press, 2005).

Eire, Carlos, *A Very Brief History of Eternity* (Princeton, NJ: Princeton University Press, 2010).

Evagrius of Pontus, *Talking Back: A Monastic Handbook for Combating Demons,* ed. David Brakke (Collegeville, MN: Cistercian Publications, 2009).

Frankl, Victor E., *Man's Search for Meaning* (New York: Pocket Books, 1984).

Geirland, John, "Go with the Flow," https://www.wired.com/1996/09/czik/.

Metropolitan Hierotheos of Nafpaktos, *Life after Death,* trans. Esther Williams (Levadia: Birth of the Theotokos Monastery, 1996).

———, *Orthodox Psychotherapy: the Science of the Fathers,* trans. Esther Williams (Levadia: Birth of the Theotokos Monastery, 2006).

———, *The Science of Spiritual Medicine: Orthodox Psychotherapy in Action,* trans. Esther Williams (Levadia: Birth of the Theotokos Monastery, 2010).

Humphries, Thomas L., *Ascetic Pneumatology from John Cassian to Gregory the Great* (Oxford: Oxford University Press, 2013).

Mack, Fr. John, *Ascending the Heights: A Layman's Guide to The Ladder of Divine Ascent* (Ben Lomond, CA: Conciliar Press, 1999), p. 73. Now out of print.

Mays, John Bentley, "Depression & Faith." Lecture, St. Silouan the Athonite Mission, Toronto, ON, February 24, 2016.

———, *In the Jaws of the Black Dogs: A Memoir of Depression* (New York: HarperCollins, 1999).

Mamalakis, Philip, "'Turning Toward' as a Pastoral Theology of Marriage," *Greek Orthodox Theological Review* 56, no. 1-4 (2011): pp. 179–195.

Meyendorff, John, *Byzantine Theology: Historical Trends and Doctrinal Themes* (New York: Fordham University Press, 1974).

Morelli, George, "Healing the Infirmity of Sin: in a Spiritual Nutshell," http://www.antiochian.org/content/healing-infirmity-sin-spiritual-nutshell.

———, "Sexual Addiction: An Orthodox and Scientific View," http://www.orthodoxytoday.org/articles6/MorelliHypersexuality.php.

Norris, Kathleen, *Acedia & Me: A Marriage, Monks, and a Writer's Life* (New York: Riverhead Books, 2008).

Nouwen, Henri J.M., *The Only Necessary Thing,* ed. Wendy Wilson Greer (New York: The Crossroad Publishing Company, 1999).

Okholm, Dennis, *Dangerous Passions, Deadly Sins: Learning from the Psychology of Ancient Monks* (Grand Rapids, MI: Brazos Press, 2014).

Pahman, Dylan, "Office Space: The Benefits of Working with Your Hands," http://humanepursuits.com/office-space/.

The Philokalia: the Complete Text, vol. 1, ed. and trans. G.E.H. Palmer, Philip Sherrard, and Kallistos Ware (New York: Faber and Faber, 1979).

Pockell, Leslie and Celia Johnson, eds., *100 Poems to Lift Your Spirits* (New York: Hachette Book Group, 2008).

Roosevelt, Theodore, "Citizenship in a Republic," http://www.theodore-roosevelt.com/trsorbonnespeech.html.

Sayers, Dorothy, "The Other Six Deadly Sins," http://www.lectionary-central.com/trinity07/Sayers.html.

Sanders, Barry, *Sudden Glory: Laughter as Subversive History* (Boston: Beacon Press, 1995).

Schaff, Philip and Henry Wallace, eds., Nicene and Post-Nicene Fathers, Second Series, vol. 11 (Buffalo, NY: Christian Literature Publishing Co., 1894). Revised and edited for New Advent by Kevin Knight, http://www.newadvent.org/fathers/3507.htm.

Schaff, Philip and Henry Wallace, eds., *Prolegomena* in Nicene and Post-Nicene Fathers, vol. 8 (New York: Cosimo Classics, 2007).

Schmemann, Alexander, *For the Life of the World: Sacraments and Orthodoxy* (Crestwood, NY: SVS Press, 2004).

———, *Great Lent: Journey to Pascha* (Crestwood, NY: SVS Press, 1969).

Sinkewicz, Robert E., ed. and trans., *Evagrius of Pontus: the Greek Ascetic Corpus* (New York: Oxford University Press, 2008).

Solomon, Andrew, *The Noonday Demon: an Atlas of Depression* (New York: Scribner, 2015).

Staniloae, Dumitru, *Eternity & Time* (Oxford: SLG Press/Fairacres Publications, 2001).

Tolstoy, Leo, *What Men Live by: And Other Tales,* trans. Aylmer Maude and Louise Shanks Maude (Auckland, New Zealand: The Floating Press, 2011).

Ware, Bishop Kallistos, Collected Works, vol. 1: *The Inner Kingdom* (Crestwood, NY: SVS Press, 2001).

Webber, Archimandrite Meletios, *Bread & Water, Wine & Oil: An Orthodox Christian Experience of God* (Ben Lomond, CA: Conciliar Press, 2007).

Notes

1   Kathleen Norris, *Acedia & Me: A Marriage, Monks, and a Writer's Life* (New York: Riverhead Books, 2008), pp. 3–4.

2   Dorothy Sayers, "The Other Six Deadly Sins," http://www.lectionarycentral.com/trinity07/Sayers.html.

3   Gabriel Bunge, *Despondency: the Spiritual Teaching of Evagrius Ponticus on Acedia* (Crestwood: St. Vladimir's Seminary Press, 2011).

4   Norris, op. cit., p. 130.

5   Alexander Schmemann, *Great Lent: Journey to Pascha* (Crestwood: St. Vladimir's Seminary Press, 1969), p. 21.

6   Schmemann, *Great Lent,* p. 34.

7   Bunge, op. cit., p. 54.

8   Evagrius, "The Practical Treatise 12," in *Evagrius of Pontus: the Greek Ascetic Corpus,* ed. and trans. Robert E. Sinkewicz (New York: Oxford University Press, 2003, 2008), p. 99.

9   Bunge, op. cit., p. 17.

10 Evagrius, "De vitiis quae opposita sunt virtutibus (On the Vices that are Opposed to the Virtues) 6," quoted in Bunge, op. cit., p. 64.

11 Evagrius, "*Epistulae* (Letters) LXII 1–2," quoted in Bunge, op. cit., p. 64.

12 Metropolitan Hierotheos of Nafpaktos, *The Science of Spiritual Medicine: Orthodox Psychotherapy in Action,* trans. Esther Williams (Levadia: Birth of the Theotokos Monastery, 2010), p. 58.

13 Robin Amis, *A Different Christianity: Early Christian Esotericism and Modern Thought* (Albany: State University of New York Press, 2003), p. 249.

14 Metropolitan Hierotheos of Nafpaktos, *Orthodox Psychotherapy: the Science of the Fathers,* trans. Esther Williams (Levadia: Birth of the Theotokos Monastery, 2006), p. 388.

15 Metropolitan Hierotheos of Nafpaktos, *Orthodox Psychotherapy,* p. 216.

16 Dennis Okholm, *Dangerous Passions, Deadly Sins: Learning from the Psychology of Ancient Monks* (Grand Rapids: Brazos Press, 2014), p. 137.

17 Metropolitan Hierotheos of Nafpaktos, *Orthodox Psychotherapy,* p. 222.

18 Schmemann, *Great Lent,* p. 24.

19 See Aquinas, *Summa Theologiae* Ia-IIae, Q 84.

20 *The Noonday Demon: an Atlas of Depression* (New York: Scribner, 2015), pp. 293–95.

21 E.g., *Conquering Depression: Heavenly Wisdom from God-Illumined Teachers* (Platina: Saint Herman Press, 1995). Though once a popular resource in Eastern Orthodox circles, this book has been put out of print in part due to its problematic conflation of depression and despondency.

22 Metropolitan Hierotheos of Nafpaktos, *Science of Spiritual Medicine*, p. 111.

23 Bunge, op. cit., p. 90.

24 Metropolitan Hierotheos of Nafpaktos, *Science of Spiritual Medicine*, p. 111.

25 Fr. George Morelli, "Sexual Addiction: An Orthodox and Scientific View," http://www.orthodoxytoday.org/articles6/MorelliHypersexuality. php.

26 John Meyendorff, *Byzantine Theology: Historical Trends and Doctrinal Themes* (New York: Fordham University Press, 1974), p. 196.

27 Fr. George Morelli, "Healing the Infirmity of Sin: in a Spiritual Nutshell," http://www.antiochian.org/content/healing-infirmity-sin-spiritual-nutshell.

28 Okholm, op. cit., p. 136.

29 Wendell Berry, *This Day: Collected & New Sabbath Poems* (Berkeley: Counterpoint, 2013), p. 183.

30 Oscar Cullman, *Christ and Time: The Primitive Christian Conception of Time* (Louisville, KY: Westminster John Knox Press, 1964), p. 61.

31 Carlos Eire, *A Very Brief History of Eternity* (Princeton: Princeton University Press, 2010), p. 7.

32 Cullman, op. cit., pp. 61–62.

33 David Bradshaw, "A Christian Approach to the Philosophy of Time," http://www.uky.edu/~dbradsh/papers/Christian%20Approach%20to%20 Phil%20of%20Time.pdf.

34 Metropolitan Hierotheos of Nafpaktos, *Life after Death*, trans. Esther Williams (Levadia: Birth of the Theotokos Monastery, 1996), pp. 45–46.

35 Kallistos Ware, Collected Works, vol. 1: *The Inner Kingdom* (Crestwood: St Vladimir's Seminary Press, 2001), p. 190.

36 Anthony Bloom, *Beginning to Pray* (New York: Paulist Press, 1970), p. 25.

37 St. Athanasius, *On the Incarnation* 3.16.

38 Ware, op. cit., p. 185.

39 Dumitru Staniloae, *Eternity & Time* (Oxford: SLG Press/ Fairacres Publications, 2001), p. 3.

40 Staniloae, op. cit., pp. 3–4.

41 Melissa Naasko, written comment to author, January 25, 2017.

42 Staniloae, op. cit., p. 5.

43 Op. cit., p. 9.

44 Ibid.

45 Op. cit., p. 8.

46 Op. cit., p. 10.

47 John Bunyan, *The Pilgrim's Progress,* ed. Roger Sharrock (Harmondsworth: Penguin Books, 1965), p. 4.

48 Ware, op. cit., pp. 181–92.

49 Staniloae, op. cit., p. 2.

50 Schmemann, *Great Lent,* p. 34.

51 Victor E. Frankl, *Man's Search for Meaning* (New York: Pocket Books, 1984), p. 86.

52 Frankl, op. cit., pp. 56–57 (emphasis Frankl's).

53 Fr. Geoffrey Ready, in conversation with the author, March 2017.

54 Ware, op. cit., p. 183; quoting C.S. Lewis.

55 St. Theophan the Recluse, quoted in *Art of Prayer: An Orthodox Anthology,* ed. Igumen Charion, trans. E. Kadloubovsky and E.M. Palmer (New York: Faber and Faber, 1997), p. 254.

56 I first encountered the connection between nepsis and the present in a series of online articles by Fr. George Morelli: "Mindfulness as Known by the Church Fathers," http://www.antiochian.org/mindfulness-known-church-fathers; "Mindfulness: a Tool to Break Bad Habits," http://www.orthodoxytoday.org/articles-2009/Morelli-Mindfullness-A-Tool-To-Break-Bad-Habits-And-Troubling-Emotions.php.

57 *The Philokalia: the Complete Text,* vol. 1, eds. and trans. G.E.H. Palmer, Philip Sherrard, and Kallistos Ware (New York: Faber and Faber, 1979), p. 539.

58 St. Hesychios the Priest, "On Watchfulness and Holiness," in *The Philokalia,* p. 224.

59 St. Theophan the Recluse, quoted in *Art of Prayer,* p. 100.

60 Note: This verse is often intoned by the deacon. It is omitted in certain dioceses or in parishes without deacons.

61 Meletios Webber, *Bread & Water, Wine & Oil: An Orthodox Christian Experience of God* (Ben Lomond: Conciliar Press, 2007), p. 19.

62 Norris, op. cit., pp. 3–4.

63 Webber, op. cit., p. 19.

64 Ibid.

65 *What Men Live by: And Other Tales,* trans. Aylmer Maude and Louise Shanks Maude (Auckland: The Floating Press, 2011), pp. 37–38.

66   Leslie Pockell and Celia Johnson, eds., *100 Poems to Lift Your Spirits* (New York: Hachette Book Group, 2008), p. 122.

67   St. John Cassian, *Institutes* 10.2, in Philip Schaff and Henry Wace, eds., Nicene and Post-Nicene Fathers, Second Series, Vol. 11 (Buffalo: Christian Literature Publishing Co., 1894), revised and edited for New Advent by Kevin Knight, http://www.newadvent.org/fathers/3507.htm.

68   St. John Cassian, *Institutes* 10.6, in Nicene and Post-Nicene Fathers; see also Evagrius, *Antirrhetikos* 6.24, in *Talking Back*.

69   Evagrius, *Antirrhetikos* 6.57, in *Talking Back*.

70   See Bunge, op. cit., p. 68.

71   Evagrius, *Capita Practica ad Anatolium* (Practical Chapters to Anatolius) 12, quoted in Bunge, op. cit., p. 76.

72   St. John Cassian, *Institutes* 10.2, in Nicene and Post-Nicene Fathers.

73   Okholm, op. cit., p. 136.

74   Evagrius, *De vitiis quae opposita sunt virtutibus* (On the Vices that are Opposed to the Virtues) 6, quoted in Bunge, op. cit., p. 64.

75   Op. cit., p. 123.

76   Ibid.

77   Op. cit, p. 54.

78   Henri J. M. Nouwen, *The Only Necessary Thing*, ed. Wendy Wilson Greer (New York: The Crossroad Publishing Company, 1999), pp. 28–29.

79   Evagrius, *Treatise to Eulogios the Monk* 9, quoted in Bunge, op. cit., p. 78.

80   Evagrius, *To Eulogios. On the Confession of Thoughts and Counsel in their Regard* 9, in *Evagrius of Pontus: the Greek Ascetic Corpus*, ed. and trans. Robert E. Sinkewicz (New York: Oxford University Press, 2008), p. 35.

81   Bunge, op. cit., p. 78.

82   Translation mine, with help from Elizabeth Wade-Sirabian.

83   Nouwen, op. cit., pp. 35–36.

84   St. Theophan the Recluse, quoted in *Art of Prayer*, p. 249.

85   Bloom, op. cit., p. 42.

86   "Citizenship in a Republic," http://www.theodore-roosevelt.com/trsorbonnespeech.html.

87   St. John of Karpathos, "For the Encouragement of the Monks in India," in *The Philokalia*, p. 464.

88   St. Theophan the Recluse, quoted in *Art of Prayer*, p. 62.

89   St. John of the Ladder, quoted in *Art of Prayer*, p. 67.

90   St. Isaac the Syrian, quoted in *Art of Prayer*, p. 118.

91   Bunge, op. cit., pp. 77–79.

92   Op. cit., p. 77.

93 Evagrius, *On the Eight Spirits of Evil* 6.16, quoted in Bunge, op. cit., p. 77.

94 St. Theophan the Recluse, quoted in *Art of Prayer*, p. 175.

95 Nouwen, op. cit., p. 108.

96 Rainer Maria Rilke, "Ich bete wieder, du erlauchter…" (translation mine, with help from Elizabeth Wade-Sirabian).

97 Philip Mamalakis, "'Turning Toward' as a Pastoral Theology of Marriage," *Greek Orthodox Theological Review* 56:1-4 (2011), pp. 179–195.

98 Mamalakis, op. cit., pp. 183–84.

99 St. Theophan the Recluse, quoted in *Art of Prayer*, p. 255.

100 This is the translation of choice favored by David Brakke for the term *antirrhetikos* (Evagrius of Pontus, *Talking Back: A Monastic Handbook for Combating Demons,* trans. David Brakke [Collegeville: Cistercian Publications, 2009], pp. 16–22).

101 For more about the reception of counter-statement, see: Brakke, David, "Introduction," in Evagrius, *Talking Back,* pp. 16–22.

102 Evagrius, *Antirrhetikos* 1.4, in *Talking Back,* p. 54.

103 Metropolitan Hierotheos of Nafpaktos, *Orthodox Psychotherapy,* p. 234.

104 Brakke, "Introduction," in Evagrius, *Talking Back,* p. 27.

105 Evagrius, *Praktikos* 27, quoted in Bunge, op. cit., p. 110.

106 Luke Dysinger, *Psalmody and Prayer in the Writing of Evagrius Ponticus* (Oxford: Oxford University Press, 2005), p. 132.

107 Bunge, op. cit., p. 110.

108 Evagrius, *Talking Back.*

109 Evagrius, *Antirrhetikos* 6.53, in *Talking Back.*

110 Bloom, op. cit., p. 43.

111 T. S. Eliot, "Little Gidding," from *Four Quartets.*

112 Evagrius, *Antirrhetikos* 6.26, in *Talking Back.*

113 Evagrius, *Antirrhetikos* 6.29, in *Talking Back.*

114 Rainer Maria Rilke, "Morning Prayer," in *The Inner Sky: Poems, Notes, Dreams,* ed. and trans. Damion Searls (Boston: David R. Godine, 2010), p. 149.

115 In *The Inner Sky,* pp. 149–151.

116 Schmemann, *Great Lent,* p. 34.

117 Evagrius, *Practical Chapters to Anatolius* 15, quoted in Bunge, op. cit., p. 102.

118 Metropolitan Anthony of Sourozh, *Essential Writings* (Maryknoll: Orbis Books, 2010), p. 74.

119 Evagrius, "On the Vices Opposed to the Virtues," in Evagrius of Pontus, p. 64.

120 Evagrius, *The Monk: A Treatise on the Practical Life* VI.28, in *Evagrius of Pontus*, p. 102.

121 Metropolitan Hierotheos of Nafpaktos, *Orthodox Psychotherapy*, p. 235.

122 John Bentley Mays, "Depression & Faith" (Lecture, St. Silouan the Athonite Mission, Toronto, ON, February 24, 2016).

123 Mays also recounted his struggle with depression in his memoir, *In the Jaws of the Black Dogs: A Memoir of Depression* (New York: HarperCollins, 1999).

124 See G.E.H. Palmer, Allyne Smith, Philip Sherrard, Kallistos Ware, eds., *Philokalia: The Eastern Christian Spiritual Texts* (Woodstock: SkyLight Paths Publishing, 2006), p. 155.

125 St. Basil the Great, quoted in Schaff, Philip, and Rev. Henry Wallace, eds., *Prolegomena*, in Nicene and Post-Nicene Fathers, vol. 8 (New York: Cosimo Classics, 2007), p. lxix.

126 Quoted in John Mack, *Ascending the Heights: A Layman's Guide to The Ladder of Divine Ascent* (Ben Lomond, CA: Conciliar Press, 1999), p. 73.

127 Evagrius, *To the Virgin* 4, in *Evagrius Ponticus*, ed. E.M. Casiday (London: Routledge, 2006), p. 168.

128 *Homilies on Genesis* 17.

129 Evagrius, *To Eulogios. On the Confession of Thoughts and Counsel in their Regard* 9, in *Evagrius of Pontus*, p. 36.

130 John Geirland, "Go with the Flow," https://www.wired.com/1996/09/czik/.

131 John G. Demakis, "Historical Precedents for Synergia: Combining Medicine, Diakonia and Sacrament in Byzantine Times," in *Raising Lazarus: Integral Healing in Orthodox Christianity,* ed. Stephen Muse (Boston: Holy Cross Orthodox Press, 2004), p. 17.

132 Thomas L. Humphries, *Ascetic Pneumatology from John Cassian to Gregory the Great* (Oxford: Oxford University Press, 2013), p. 184.

133 Dylan Pahman, "Office Space: The Benefits of Working with Your Hands," http://humanepursuits.com/office-space/.

134 Sadly, this talk no longer seems to be online and I do not remember its original title.

135 David Athey, "The Theological Necessity for Humor," https://incommunion.org/2004/12/12/the-theological-necessity-for-humor/.

136 Barry Sanders, *Sudden Glory: Laughter as Subversive History* (Boston: Beacon Press, 1995), p. 62.

137 Athey, op. cit.

138 Alexander Schmemann, *For the Life of the World: Sacraments and Ortho-*

doxy (Crestwood: St. Vladimir's Seminary Press, 2004), pp. 37–38.

139 I am grateful to have been reminded of this "in the nick of time" by the eloquent Fr. Geoffrey Ready (lecture, Resurrection of the Logos Panel Discussion, Toronto, ON, March 7, 2017).

140 Nouwen, op. cit., p. 105.

141 William Shakespeare, *Macbeth* 5.5.

About the Author

D R. NICOLE ROCCAS has been researching and writing about time from both a historical and theological perspective for nearly ten years. In addition to being a writer and editor, she lectures at the Orthodox School of Theology at Trinity College (Toronto). You can find more of her writing on her Ancient Faith podcast and blog, *Time Eternal,* and her website, www. nicoleroccas.com. Nicole has a PhD in History from the University of Cincinnati.

A native of Wisconsin, Nicole lives in Toronto with her husband, Basil, whose efforts to indoctrinate her into the ways of maple syrup and Canadian spelling have yet to take effect.

Listen to Nicole on
www.ancientfaith.com

Time Eternal explores the beautiful and the difficult aspects of time on this earth. The various episodes touch on how our experience and perception of time can become distorted because of sin and brokenness, and how the message of Christ and our Orthodox faith can help restore and resurrect the way we live with time.

Also from Ancient Faith Publishing

Everywhere Present: Christianity in a One-Storey Universe
by Fr. Stephen Freeman
Have you ever referred to God as "the Man upstairs"? Most Christians living in a secular society have unwittingly relegated God and all things spiritual to the "second storey" of the universe: a realm we cannot reach except through death. The effect of this is to banish God, along with the saints and angels, from our everyday lives.

In *Everywhere Present,* popular blogger and podcaster Fr. Stephen Freeman makes a compelling case for becoming aware of God's living and active presence in every moment of our lives here and now. Learning to practice your Christian faith in a one-storey universe will change your life—and make possible the living, intimate relationship with God you've always dreamed of.

Becoming a Healing Presence
by Albert S. Rossi, PhD, with a foreword by Fr. Thomas Hopko
In order to become a healing presence for others, we must first be healed ourselves—through an active relationship with the great Healer, Christ. Drawing on the teachings of the Fathers and saints of the Church, Dr. Rossi gently points the way toward deepening our love for God and for each other so that others may experience Christ through us.

Ancient Faith Publishing hopes you have enjoyed and benefited from this book. The proceeds from the sales of our books only partially cover the costs of operating our nonprofit ministry—which includes both the work of **Ancient Faith Publishing** and the work of **Ancient Faith Radio**. Your financial support makes it possible to continue this ministry both in print and online. Donations are tax-deductible and can be made at **www.ancientfaith.com.**

To view our other publications,
log onto our website: **store.ancientfaith.com**

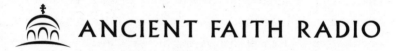 **ANCIENT FAITH RADIO**

Bringing you Orthodox Christian music, readings, prayers, teaching, and podcasts 24 hours a day since 2004 at **www.ancientfaith.com**